Hot and Spicy
and Meatless

Also by Dave DeWitt

Hot Spots
Just North of the Border (with Nancy Gerlach)
The Food Lover's Handbook to the Southwest (with Mary Jane Wilan)
Fiery Appetizers (with Nancy Gerlach)
New Mexico
Chile Peppers: A Selected Bibliography of the Capsicums
Callaloo, Calypso, and Carnival (with Mary Jane Wilan)
The Fiery Cuisines (with Nancy Gerlach)
The Whole Chile Pepper Book (with Nancy Gerlach)
A World of Curries (with Arthur Pais)
The Pepper Garden (with Paul Bosland)

How to Order:

Single copies may be ordered from Prima Publishing, P.O. Box 1260BK, Rocklin, CA 95677; telephone (916) 786-0426. Quantity discounts are also available. On your letterhead, include information concerning the intended use of the books and the number of books you wish to purchase.

▼▲▼▲▼▲▼▲▼▲▼▲▼▲▼▲▼

Hot and Spicy and Meatless

Over 150 Delicious, Fiery, and Healthful Recipes

Dave DeWitt

Mary Jane Wilan

Melissa T. Stock

Prima Publishing
P.O. Box 1260BK
Rocklin, CA 95677
(916) 786-0426

Production by Robin Lockwood, Bookman Productions
Copyediting by Judith Abrahms
Composition by Janet Hansen, Alphatype
Interior design by Suzanne Montazer and Renee Deprey
Cover design by The Dunlavey Studio, Sacramento

Portions of this book first appeared in *Chile Pepper* magazine. Used by permission.

Library of Congress Cataloging-in-Publication Data

DeWitt, Dave.
    Hot and spicy and meatless : over 150 delicious, fiery, and healthful recipes / by Dave DeWitt.
        p.   cm.
    Includes index.
    ISBN 1-55958-361-4
    1. Vegetarian cookery.   2. Spices.   3. Condiments.   I. Title.
TX837.D39   1994
641.5'636—dc20   93-8070
                                                                          CIP

94 95 96 97 98 RRD 10 9 8 7 6 5 4

Printed in the United States of America

To all the readers of
Chile Pepper *magazine*
who have supported us
over the years.

▼▲▼▲▼▲▼▲▼▲▼▲▼▲▼▲▼▲▼▲

ACKNOWLEDGMENTS

Our thanks to Jennifer Basye, who had the idea, and to the other fine people who helped us out: Nanette Blanchard, Cindy Castillo, Jeff Corydon, Jeanette DeAnda, Donald Downes, Marta and Alan Figel, Nancy Gerlach, Ignacio Griego, Sr., Antonio Heras-Duran, Sharon Hudgins, Jeffree Wyn Itrich, Arthur Krochmal, W. C. Longacre, Arthur Pais, Jim Peyton, Rosa Rajkovic, Judith Ritter, Clara Sanchez, Todd Sanson, Robert Spiegel, Richard Sterling, Jill Sullivan, Robb Walsh, Adelina Willem, and Kurt Zuger.

▼△▼△▼△▼△▼△▼△▼△▼△▼△▼

CONTENTS

INTRODUCTION

We've eliminated the meat, increased the heat, and marched to a healthy beat in this cookbook. Our concept was simple from the beginning: collect and create hot and spicy recipes where meat was simply not a factor and was therefore not included. Meats and meat products eliminated here include red meats, poultry, fish, shellfish, and all stocks and gravies made from them. We have included dairy products such as milk and cheese, but have described the many kinds of non-dairy substitutes — as well as meat substitutes — in Appendix A.

We do not profess to be vegetarians — in fact, we like a wide variety of foods from around the world. But hot and spicy food lends itself to the absence of meat because of the intense flavors and sensations produced by the chiles. This regimen also works perfectly with low-salt, low-cholesterol, and low-fat diets, and so the recipes reflect these health considerations as much as possible without totally sacrificing flavor. In Appendix A we cover the health benefits of chile peppers in detail, such as their ability to burn calories, their high vitamin content, and the fact that they are low in sodium and fat.

A personal note: All of us are cooks and writers who have teamed up to combine our experiences in hot and spicy cuisines. Dave is the editor of *Chile Pepper* magazine and the author, or co-author, of numerous books on fiery foods; Mary Jane Wilan is married to Dave and has co-authored two other books with him; Melissa T. Stock is the associate editor of *Chile Pepper* magazine and the author of numerous food articles.

During the past two decades of our immersion in the field of chile peppers, we have collected and tested historic recipes, created various dishes, borrowed recipes from our friends, and taken notes on our experiences of cooking with chile peppers. We have also relied on our far-flung correspondents for the magazine to provide hot and spicy and meatless creations from around the world.

In this book, we have combined these experiences with anecdotes, facts, and miscellaneous tidbits that we've collected over the years to spice up the recipes even more. They cover a wide range of topics from healthful food habits and trends, to fascinating facts about chiles and the other ingredients, to philosophical speculations about hot and spicy foods and their influence on our lives. For readers who are devoted to chile peppers, we have included a discussion of the numerous varieties in Appendix B and a brief lesson on how to grow your own chile garden in Appendix C.

A note on the heat scale. We've used the same mild, medium, hot, and extremely hot ratings for the recipes that have been running in *Chile Pepper* magazine for years now. They are based on our own tastes, taking into consideration the type of chile in the recipe and the amount of it that is used. Cooks who wish to increase or decrease heat levels based on these ratings can easily adjust the amount of chile.

To subscribe to *Chile Pepper* magazine, write to P.O. Box 80780, Albuquerque, NM 87198 or call (800) 9595-HOT (959-5468).

Key Recipes, Salsas, and Sauces

T he first recipes in this chapter are basic ones. They are called for throughout the book. They are Rich Vegetable Stock, Chile-Infused Oil, Pickled Chiles, Ketchup with a Kick, Herbal-Chile Salt Substitute, Sherry Pepper Vinegar, Spicy Red Wine Vinegar, and Simple Seitan.

Salsas and sauces consist of the pure essences of chiles and the other ingredients they are combined with. Other than eating chiles raw, the simplest recipe for using the pungent pods is to crush them into liquid form. Undoubtedly, then, hot sauces have been around as long as the chiles themselves, although they were not bottled until long after Columbus arrived in the New World. Like the chiles, hot sauces spread rapidly around the globe, and today there are hundreds of brands, including many in Asia.

Dave and Mary Jane have collected hot sauces on their travels all over the world for their friends who are serious hot-sauce collectors. There are many brands of hot sauces in the Caribbean and in Louisiana, but the largest display of sauces they ever encountered was in Johore Baru, Malaysia. In a supermarket there, they photographed a rack of sauces fully seven feet high and twenty feet long, containing hundreds of different brands of hot sauces.

It is important to differentiate among hot sauces, picante sauces, and salsas. Generally speaking, hot sauces are made with chiles and water or vinegar, plus herbs, spices, and occasionally fruits and vegetables. The ingredients are sometimes cooked, but always are liquefied, and the consistency of the hot sauces is usually quite thin.

Picante sauces are processed (and often crushed or cooked) combinations of chiles, tomatoes, and onions, and are much thicker than hot sauces. Salsas are thicker still, and consist of discernible chunks of chiles and vegetables (or fruits) mixed together but not crushed or cooked.

Cooked sauces are not used as condiments, but rather as an integral part of the main course, particularly in Mexico and the American Southwest. They are used to top main dishes such as pastas, or they are incorporated into the entree, as in enchiladas.

Nearly every variety of chile grown commercially is used in some sort of sauce or salsa. In the United States, the favorite chiles for sauces have long been Tabasco, New Mexican, jalapeño, and serrano. But during the past few years, the habanero has taken the U.S. by storm. Used mostly in liquefied hot sauces, the habanero is beloved because of its extreme heat and its unique, fruity flavor.

A well-known West Indian legend tells of a Creole woman who loved habaneros so much that she decided to make a soup out of them. She reasoned that since the chiles were so good in other foods, a soup made entirely of habaneros would be heavenly. But after her children tasted the broth, they ran to the river to cool their mouths. Unfortunately, they drank so much water that they drowned — heavenly indeed! The moral of the story is that you must be careful with habaneros, which is why many sauce companies combine them with vegetables or fruits to dilute the heat.

In this chapter we have grouped the sauces into their natural categories, including condiments, salsas, cooked sauces, pasta sauces, relishes, and chutneys. The condiments include our recipe for a typical Caribbean Hot Pepper Sauce and also one with an interesting twist, West Indies Ginger Pepper Sauce. Then we journey to Southeast Asia for Thai Peanut Sauce with Red Chile. Two other hot sauces round out the condiment category: L'Exotic Sauce Dynamite, from Madagascar via Montreal, and Xcatic Sauce, from the Yucatan Peninsula.

The commonest fresh salsa made in the United States is variously called "salsa cruda," "salsa fria," or "salsa fresca." It consists of serrano or jalapeño chiles, tomatoes, onions, garlic, and cilantro all chopped up together. Thinner versions of it are bottled as "picante sauces." We have included an interesting variation on it, Three Amigos Salsa, featuring three different kinds of peppers. Another version, from northern Mexico, is Salsa de Jalapeño en Escabeche (Pickled Jalapeño Salsa).

We begin our cooked sauces with Creamy Horseradish Sauce, which combines hot paprika with horseradish and is used as a topping for vegetables. The next four sauces come from New Mexico, where sauces have become an art form. Classic New Mexico Red Chile Sauce is a basic sauce used in Southwestern versions of Mexican food, and Quick Red Chile Mole Sauce is a New Mexican variation on a classic chocolate-chile sauce from central Mexico. Salsa de Chile Verde (Classic New Mexican Green Chile Sauce) is used in cooking in the same way as the red sauces. Santa Fe Exotix's Excellent Green Chile Sauce is chef Todd Sanson's award-winning version of the classic New Mexican green sauce.

Our pasta sauces reveal interesting combinations of ingredients. Cilantro and Piñon Pesto for Pasta combines Southwestern and Mexican ingredients — cilantro and piñon nuts — and 911 Tomato-Basil Sauce with Habaneros shows how the world's hottest peppers can liven up a tomato sauce. Pungent Puttanesca Sauce is considerably milder and is flavored with black olives and capers.

Relishes and chutneys are actually just thick sauces, and we've uncovered quite a collection of them. Cranberry-Habanero Relish features two unlikely ingredients mixed together, but the taste is great. Carrots, ginger, cucumbers, and mint are combined to create the Asian-flavored Hot and Sour Serrano-Carrot Relish, and A Gardener's Select Relish combines fruits with jalapeños. Two chutneys round out the thick sauces: Madras Mango Chutney from India and Dos Chiles Verdes Chutney, featuring an interesting combination of tomatoes, tomatillos, raisins, and two different chiles.

   To complete the chapter, we offer four additional condiments made with chiles and other ingredients: Hot Horseradish Mustard, Fennel-Dill Mustard Sauce, Limon Tarragon Marinade, and Mexican Mayonnaise. The first three condiments can be used to top or to marinate vegetables, and the Mexican Mayonnaise is great on sandwiches.

RICH VEGETABLE STOCK

This stock is good enough to serve as a first-course consommé, in addition to using it as a basis for some of the other recipes in this cookbook. Sautéing the vegetables before adding the water gives an additional richness to the stock. If you wish, adding a 1- to 2-inch piece of kombu seaweed will add a further depth of flavor. This stock will keep for two days, covered, in the refrigerator. It can also be frozen; divide it into 2- or 3-cup freezer containers. The jalapeños are optional for making the stock spicy.

2 **tablespoons high-quality olive oil**	1 **teaspoon dried marjoram**
2 **large ribs of celery, including the leaves, cut into 1-inch pieces**	½ **cup chopped button mushrooms**
2 **carrots, coarsely chopped**	1 **zucchini, peeled and sliced**
1 **large onion, chopped**	3 **cups coarsely chopped tomatoes**
2 **leeks, chopped (white part only)**	3 **jalapeño chiles, seeds and stems removed, chopped (optional)**
3 **green onions**	
3 **garlic cloves, peeled**	10 **cups cold water**
⅓ **cup chopped parsley, including the stems**	5 **whole black peppercorns**
¼ **cup fresh chopped basil (or 2 tablespoons dried basil)**	

Heat the olive oil in a large Dutch oven. Add the celery and the carrots and sauté for a minute; then add the remaining ingredients (except the water and peppercorns) and sauté for 5 minutes.

Add the cold water and the peppercorns and bring the mixture to a boil. Then lower the heat to a simmer, cover, and cook for 2 hours. Remove the cover and simmer for another 30 minutes. Strain the stock through a fine strainer and salt to taste.

Yield: 6 to 8 cups

CHILE-INFUSED OIL

This spicy oil can be substituted for any vegetable oil in any of the recipes in this book, or used in place of the oils in other recipes to fire up those dishes. It's great with stir-fries! The longer the chiles steep, the hotter the oil will be. We keep the same bottle for years and just add oil as needed — the chiles keep on going, and going, and going.

1 quart vegetable oil (such as peanut, olive, or safflower)	**1½ cups small dried hot chiles such as piquins or santakas**

Heat the oil in a saucepan until it just starts to smoke. Add the chiles, remove from the heat, transfer to a glass container, and let steep for at least 8 hours. Strain the oil through a fine sieve or cloth, leaving the chiles inside the bottle.

Yield: 1 quart
Heat Scale: Medium to Hot

The Love Apple

Tomatoes, one of the principal ingredients in many salsas, were once thought to be an aphrodisiac. As tomato expert Fred DuBose explains, this was "perhaps on the puritanical assumption that anything that looked so alluring — so smooth, round, and scarlet — had to have, like Eve's apple, a wicked side." One of the first names of the tomato in Italy was *pomum amoris,* the apple of love, and its first English name was *love apple.* "But the first to call it that," according to DuBose, "probably did so more for the beautiful flame-red color of the fruit than for any amatory qualities."

PICKLED CHILES

This recipe, from *Chile Pepper* food editor Nancy Gerlach, helped out our magazine's readers. She wrote, "Every year at harvest time, we receive numerous requests for pickled chile recipes. So here is a basic recipe that can be used for pickling vegetables such as carrots and cauliflower as well as chiles. This will pickle approximately two pounds of ripe chiles."

THE BRINE AND THE CHILES

1   cup pickling salt

3   cups water

2   pounds ripe chiles of your choice

Combine the salt and water and cover the chiles with the mixture. Place a plate on the chiles to keep them submerged in the brine. Soak the chiles overnight to crisp them. Drain, rinse well, and dry.

PICKLING SOLUTION

3   cups 4 to 5 percent distilled white vinegar

3   cups water

3   teaspoons pickling salt

Poke a couple of holes in the top of each chile to keep them from floating in the liquid. Pack the chiles tightly in sterilized jars.

Combine the vinegar, water, and salt. Bring the solution to a boil and pour over the chiles, leaving ¼ inch of liquid above them. Gently tap the side of the jar to remove any trapped bubbles.

Store for 4 to 6 weeks before serving.

Yield: 4 pints

Heat Scale: Varies according to the variety of chile used

KETCHUP WITH A KICK

This recipe was given to us by Jeffree Wyn Itrich, author of *Spice It Up!* (Border Books, 1993). Jeffree is a fine, creative cook. She tries to plant a small garden every year, including herbs and lots of tomatoes. Malt vinegar is an integral ingredient in this recipe, but she says, "Many malt vinegars do not contain a high enough acidity level for proper canning. Hence, I suggest you refrigerate this ketchup instead, since a more acidic vinegar would alter the flavor."

6	pounds ripe tomatoes, chopped		Dash of white pepper
1	small purple onion, peeled and chopped	1/2	teaspoon habanero powder (or more to taste)
2	teaspoons dried chervil or parsley	1	cinnamon stick, halved
1 1/2	cups malt vinegar	1/2	whole nutmeg, split by tapping carefully with a hammer
1/2	cup plus 2 tablespoons packed brown sugar		
3/4	teaspoon salt	1/2	teaspoon mustard seeds
		1	teaspoon fennel seeds

Place the tomatoes, onion, and chervil or parsley in a heavy 4- to 5-quart pot. Bring the ingredients to a boil over high heat, reduce the heat to medi-um, and cook until the tomatoes are softened, about 20 to 25 minutes.

Press the tomato mixture through a fine sieve, pressing hard on the solids with the back of a broad wooden spoon to release the puree. Return the puree to the pot and discard the solids.

Add the vinegar, sugar, salt, white pepper, and powdered habanero chile to the puree. Tie the remaining ingredients in several layers of cheesecloth and add them to the pot. Bring the mixture to a boil over high heat, reduce the heat to medium, and cook 2 to 2 1/2 hours, uncovered. As it cooks, periodically remove the froth that rises and stir down the sides. When the mixture is very thick, remove the tied spices.

Ladle the ketchup into a jar. Allow it to cool, then refrigerate. It keeps indefinitely.

Yield: 2 1/2 cups
Heat Scale: Medium

HERBAL-CHILE SALT SUBSTITUTE

Use this recipe to eliminate excess salt from your diet, or salt from any recipe in this cookbook. It tastes best, of course, when you grow and dry your own herbs, but commercially purchased dried herbs will work well. Try this mixture on baked potatoes, pasta, and vegetables — and especially on corn on the cob.

4 tablespoons dried parsley
4 tablespoons dried basil
2 teaspoons dried rosemary
1 tablespoon dried tarragon
2 tablespoons dried thyme
1 tablespoon dried dill weed

2 tablespoons paprika
1 teaspoon celery seed
1 teaspoon crushed, dried red chiles such as piquins, or 2 teaspoons New Mexican red chile powder

Place all ingredients in a mini–food processor and blend for 10 seconds or so. Put the mixture into a shaker jar and cover tightly until ready to use.

Yield: ½ cup
Heat Scale: Mild to medium

Note: Try adding 1 tablespoon of pineapple-sage to replace the tarragon.

SHERRY PEPPER VINEGAR

This recipe is easy to make and can be used any time you would normally use a vinegar, for a very unusual taste. Buy a good dry sherry to start with. The amount you make varies according to the size of the bottle you use for the process. Remember that the mouth of the bottle has to be large enough for the peppers, and if the cover is metallic, make sure you put some plastic wrap over the top of the bottle before you screw the top on. Fresh or dried chiles may be used; if using fresh chiles, slice them in half and remove the seeds and stems.

1   **sterile glass bottle**
4   **to 5 assorted hot chiles
    (such as chiltepin, piquin,
    serrano, or habanero)**

1   **bottle (750 milliliters)
    good-quality dry sherry**

Place the chiles in the sterile bottle and fill with the sherry up to within
1 inch of the top. Drink the rest of the sherry if you like. Cover the top
of the bottle with plastic wrap and then add a more secure cover. Store
in a cool, dark place for 30 days, shaking occasionally. Use it creatively!

Yield: 1 bottle
Heat Scale: Varies according to the number and
type of chiles used and the length of time they steep

∿∿∿∿∿∿∿∿∿∿∿∿

SPICY RED WINE VINEGAR

Many creative chefs have herb gardens. An herb garden doesn't need
to be large or elaborate to produce fresh herbs, which are such a treat;
extra herbs can be microwaved until dried and stored for later. Once
you get hooked on making different herbal vinegars, you'll want to
expand your knowledge of herb gardening.

¾   **cup fresh basil sprigs,
    washed and patted dry**
3   **to 7 small hot red chiles
    (such as piquin or
    chiltepin), depending on
    your desired heat level**

1   **pint of good-quality red
    wine vinegar**
1   **non-metallic bottle,
    slightly larger than a pint**

Place the basil and the chiles in a non-metallic saucepan. Pour in the vinegar and heat, but do not boil. Let the mixture cool slightly and pour it into the non-metallic bottle. Cover the top loosely (again, nothing metallic) and let the mixture steep for 10 days.

Yield: slightly more than 1 pint
Heat Scale: Varies with the number of chiles

▼▲▼▲▼▲▼▲▼▲▼▲▼▲▼▲▼▲▼

Food Habits of the '90s?

The Zagat Survey, which publishes restaurant reviews and ratings written by consumers in larger American cities, asked 8,500 diners in New York and Los Angeles to complete the following phrase: "The food trends of the '90s will be . . ." The following responses may seem strange, but as copublisher Tim Zagat noted, "Remember, ten years ago, if you told most people that goat cheese, blue corn, and squid-blackened pasta would be among the hot foods to try in the 1990s, they would have looked at you sideways." Here are the consumers' suggestions about what will be the trendy foods of the next decade: artichoke oil, designer ketchup, Caribbean "jerk" foods, Russian-Cambodian cuisine, South African soul food, light kosher cuisine, haute Spanish food, bistro Oriental, all–oat bran meal, rainforest cooking, macrobiotic African cuisine, sugar-cane juice, South American fruit stews, and New Guinea beetroot.

SIMPLE SEITAN

Use this recipe to prepare seitan for other recipes presented in later chapters. Freeze the unused portions.

1 cup instant gluten flour (vital wheat germ)	**6 cups Rich Vegetable Stock (see recipe, p. 5)**
⅞ cup water	

Completely combine the flour and water in a bowl. Knead the mixture for a minute to blend. Divide into 16 to 20 large balls, stretching and pressing into cutlet shape.

Pour the vegetable stock into a large pot. Drop the cutlets into the broth and simmer on low for about 50 minutes. Drain and cool before using.

Yield: 3 cups seitan

Exotic Bravado

"Chiles are a lifestyle. It's an urban cowboy idea of bravado. You have a sense of machismo without running around with a gunrack in the back of your truck. There's got to be a way of proving one's bravado. Chiles are one way of doing that. Chiles will become more popular everywhere. People want—and need—a sense of exoticness."

—Mark Miller, quoted in the *El Paso Times,* April 26, 1992

CARIBBEAN HOT PEPPER SAUCE

Throughout the Caribbean, variations of this basic hot-sauce recipe can be found. The sauce is far superior to many of the bottled ones and takes only a few minutes to make. We love to add it to soups and stews. Its uses are endless; true believers even take it on vacation with them!

1 cup minced shallots

2 garlic cloves, minced

1 habanero chile, seeds and stem removed, minced (or substitute 3 jalapeño or serrano chiles)

2 tablespoons olive oil

½ teaspoon salt

3 tablespoons fresh lime juice

⅔ cup boiling water

Combine the first five ingredients, then stir in the lime juice and the boiling water. Let the sauce stand for at least an hour. Stir thoroughly before using. Store in a glass jar in the refrigerator.

Yield: 1½ cups
Heat Scale: Hot

WEST INDIES GINGER PEPPER SAUCE

This recipe comes from W. C. Longacre, owner of W. C.'s Mountain Road Cafe in Albuquerque. He says of his cooking style, "From my background in cooking in New Mexico, Hong Kong, and Florida, I invented what I call New-Hong-Key cuisine. It's my interpretation of the combining of the foods of those three regions." Use it as a relish or as an unusual dressing for greens.

¼ teaspoon salt

2 tablespoons cornstarch

¼ cup sugar

¼ cup fresh lime juice

¼ cup unsweetened pineapple juice

1 cup water

1 teaspoon soy sauce

2 tablespoons minced fresh ginger

2 tablespoons minced jalapeño chile

1 teaspoon cayenne powder

½ cup fresh pineapple chunks, or, if using canned fruit, pineapple in natural juices

2 tablespoons chardonnay or any dry white wine

1 tablespoon chopped fresh cilantro

In a small saucepan, blend the salt, cornstarch, sugar, lime juice, and pineapple juice until smooth.

Gradually stir in the water, soy sauce, ginger, jalapeño, and cayenne. Cook over medium heat, stirring constantly until the sauce is thick and transparent.

Finish the sauce by stirring in the pineapple chunks, white wine, and cilantro. Use the sauce warm.

Yield: 1½ to 2 cups
Heat Scale: Hot

〰〰〰〰〰〰〰〰〰

THAI PEANUT SAUCE WITH RED CHILE

This classic sauce is traditionally served over white rice cooked with 1 tablespoon of minced lemongrass. Accompany it with a salad from Chapter 3, or serve it over a cucumber salad garnished with fresh cilantro.

1 tablespoon peanut oil
1 tablespoon red chile paste (available in Asian markets)
3 cloves of garlic, minced
2 tablespoons tomato paste
½ cup Rich Vegetable Stock (see recipe, p. 5)
½ teaspoon honey

1 tablespoon smooth peanut butter
¼ cup hoisin sauce (available in Asian markets)
¼ cup ground unsalted peanuts
2 teaspoons New Mexican red chile powder

Heat the oil in a saucepan. When the oil is hot, add the chile paste and garlic and cook for about 30 seconds, stirring constantly. Keep the heat at medium and whisk in the tomato paste, vegetable stock, honey, peanut butter, and hoisin sauce. Bring to a boil until thickened, whisking constantly. Remove from the heat and stir in the ground peanuts and chile powder. Serve warm.

Yield: About 1 cup (2 servings)
Heat Scale: Medium

‸‸‸‸‸‸‸‸‸‸‸‸‸

L'EXOTIC SAUCE DYNAMITE

From *Chile Pepper* magazine's Montreal correspondent, Judith Ritter, comes a typical Madagascar-style sauce that she collected at the Restaurant L'Exotic. Judith profiled the restaurant for *Chile Pepper* and notes that the sauce is served with most entrees at L'Exotic. Add it to soups or stews.

12 "bird" chiles (chiltepins
    or piquins), crushed
3   tablespoons freshly
    ground ginger root
3   tablespoons freshly
    ground garlic
1   medium onion, diced

1/4 cup tomato paste
1   cup white vinegar
2   teaspoons salt
1   cup water
1   tablespoon freshly
    chopped thyme

Mix all the ingredients together in a pan. Bring to a boil, then reduce
heat and simmer for 15 minutes. Remove the sauce from the heat, cool,
puree in a blender, and place in a small jar. It keeps for up to a year in
the refrigerator.

Yield: 2 cups
Heat Scale: Hot

∿∿∿∿∿∿∿∿∿∿∿

SALSA XCATIC

This tasty recipe was collected for us by Marta and Alan Figel, owners
of On the Verandah restaurant in Highlands, North Carolina. Marta
was on assignment for *Chile Pepper* magazine at the time, and she later
described the principal chile in this salsa: "The Yucatan is identified
with its native fiery chile, the habanero, and the lesser-known chile
xcatic (pronounced *sch-KA-tik*). Similar to a chile guero, it is pale green,
much hotter, and resembles the New Mexican chile in shape and size."

9   *xcatic* chiles, stems and
    seeds removed, finely
    chopped (or substitute
    yellow wax hot or guero
    chiles)
1   medium white onion,
    finely chopped

1/4 cup vegetable oil
1/2 teaspoon salt
2   tablespoons white
    vinegar
    Freshly ground black
    pepper to taste

Sauté the chiles and onion in the oil for 20 minutes at low heat. Place in a blender with the remaining ingredients and puree until smooth.

Yield: 1 cup
Heat Scale: Medium

∿∿∿∿∿∿∿∿∿∿∿

THREE AMIGOS SALSA

This salsa was given its name for two reasons: First, it's so good that it only takes the three of us to finish it off; second, it contains the perfect blend of three peppers—serrano, yellow bell pepper, and a bit of habanero. Eat it with chips or spread it over crackers.

1   red bell pepper
1   serrano chile, seeds and stem removed, chopped
¼   habanero chile, seeds and stem removed, chopped (1 teaspoon of dried habanero powder may be substituted)
1   tablespoon chopped cilantro

2   tablespoons chopped black olives
2   tablespoons olive oil
1   clove garlic, minced
½   teaspoon cumin
1   teaspoon lemon juice
1   tablespoon dark Mexican beer

Roast the bell pepper over an open flame until it is completely charred. Cool to room temperature, peel, seed, and cut into ¼-inch-wide strips about the length of your thumb. In a bowl, combine the bell pepper, serrano, habanero, cilantro, olives, olive oil, garlic, and cumin. Mix well and let stand covered for at least 1 hour for the flavors to blend. Add the lemon juice and dark Mexican beer, stir well, and serve.

Serves: 3
Heat Scale: Medium

SALSA DE JALAPEÑO EN ESCABECHE (PICKLED JALAPEÑO SAUCE)

Jim Peyton, who travels in Mexico reporting for *Chile Pepper* magazine and gathering material for his cookbooks (such as *El Norte: The Cuisine of Northern Mexico*), collected this sauce in Durango. It makes an excellent table sauce and is good with tostados. He says that using the pickled jalapeño may violate strictures against canned ingredients, but that they add a unique flavor that works well with the other components in the sauce.

1½ **teaspoons olive oil**

2   **cloves garlic, minced**

2   **to 3 pickled jalapeños, minced**

1½ **tablespoons juice from the can or jar of jalapeños**

3   **medium tomatoes, broiled over an open flame until charred, and finely chopped, including the peel**

¾   **teaspoon oregano**

¼   **teaspoon salt**

⅓   **cup minced onion**

Heat the olive oil in a small saucepan and add the garlic. Sauté over a very low heat until the garlic is soft but not browned—1 to 2 minutes.

Add the remaining ingredients, stirring to mix well. Bring the sauce to a boil, then turn down the heat and simmer, uncovered, for 5 minutes. Allow to cool before serving.

Yield: 2 cups

Heat Scale: Hot

CREAMY HORSERADISH SAUCE

This basic sauce from Hungary is used to spice up steamed vegetables, such as broccoli, beets, and carrots, and can even be used to liven up baked potatoes or summer squash.

2 tablespoons margarine	⅓ cup peeled and grated horseradish
2 tablespoons flour	
¼ teaspoon salt	½ cup low-fat milk
1 teaspoon hot paprika	
1 cup Rich Vegetable Stock (see recipe, p. 5)	

Melt the margarine in a saucepan and stir in the flour, salt, and paprika. Cook for two minutes, but do not allow the flour to brown. Stir in the broth and horseradish, then heat. Slowly add the low-fat milk, stirring constantly. Cook over low heat until smooth and thickened.

Yield: 1½ cups
Heat Scale: Mild

〰〰〰〰〰〰〰

CLASSIC NEW MEXICO RED CHILE SAUCE

We continue to pass along the New Mexico chile sauces in book after book because they are so superior to "chile gravies" used with enchiladas in other parts of the country. This basic sauce can be used in any recipe calling for a red sauce, including either traditional Mexican or New Southwestern versions of beans, tacos, tamales, and enchiladas. Spices such as cumin, coriander, and Mexican oregano may be added to taste. Some versions of this sauce call for the onion and garlic to be sautéed in vegetable oil before the chiles and water are added.

10	**to 12 dried whole red New Mexican chiles**	**3**	**cloves garlic, chopped**
1	**large onion, chopped**	**3**	**cups water**

Place the chiles on a baking pan; place in a 250-degree oven for about 10 to 15 minutes or until the chiles smell as if they are toasted, taking care not to let them burn. Remove the stems and seeds and crumble them into a saucepan.

Add the remaining ingredients, bring to a boil, reduce the heat, and simmer for 20 to 30 minutes.

Puree the mixture in a blender until smooth and strain if necessary. If the sauce is too thin, place it back on the stove and simmer until it is reduced to the desired consistency.

Yield: 2 to 2½ cups
Heat Scale: Medium

The Largest Hot Sauce Collection

A sidebar on the hot and spicy movement should include those aficionados who have dedicated their lives to collecting commercial bottled hot sauces from around the world. In June 1993, Chuck Evans of Powell, Ohio, with his collection of more than 800 different sauces, was supplanted as the top collector in the country by Chip Hearn of Dewey Beach, Delaware, whose collection exceeds 1,100. Chip and his father spend their holidays traveling to exotic corners of the world to collect hot sauces.

QUICK RED CHILE MOLE SAUCE

This sauce is what chef Todd Sanson refers to as "mock mole" because it is his fast version of the famous Mexican sauce. Todd is a culinary instructor at Santa Fe Community College; in his spare time, he creates his own line of spicy salsas and condiments, called Santa Fe Exotix. This sauce can be used in enchiladas and is served with Todd's Tofu-Stuffed Poblanos (see recipe, p. 155).

2 tablespoons vegetable oil

1 medium onion, diced

2 cloves garlic, minced

2 cups Rich Vegetable Stock (see recipe, p. 5) or water

⅔ cup New Mexican red chile powder

½ cup ancho chile powder

1½ rounds Ibarra Mexican chocolate (no substitutions)

3 tablespoons ground Mexican cinnamon (canela), or use stick cinnamon

Salt to taste

Heat the oil, then sauté the onions and garlic for 5 minutes, or until tender.

Heat up the stock or water and when it is near to boiling, add the chile powders and stir for a minute or two. Then turn down the heat to medium.

Place the chocolate in a large plastic bag and crush it coarsely with a hammer. Add the chocolate to the chile-stock pot. Stir until it is melted.

Then add the cinnamon and the sautéed onion-garlic mixture to the pot. Simmer for 20 minutes or until the sauce begins to thicken, stirring occasionally.

Yield: 2½ cups
Heat Scale: Medium

SALSA DE CHILE VERDE
(CLASSIC NEW MEXICO
GREEN CHILE SAUCE)

This is also a classic New Mexico sauce, and everyone you meet in the state has his or her own special version. The green chile, onions, and garlic are the three ingredients that remain constant. The tomatoes and tomatillos are not necessarily traditional in New Mexico, but they make a tasty addition. The sauce can be pureed for a smoother texture if desired. It can be poured over hash-browned potatoes, or used for enchiladas, tacos, and burritos—all meatless, of course.

2 tablespoons vegetable oil	2 tomatillos, peeled, seeded, and finely diced (optional)
1 large onion, finely chopped	2 tablespoons chopped cilantro
2 cloves garlic, minced	½ teaspoon ground cumin
6 or 7 New Mexican green chiles, roasted, peeled, seeds and stems removed, and diced	½ teaspoon ground coriander
1 large red tomato, peeled, seeded, and diced (optional)	1½ cups Rich Vegetable Stock (see recipe, p. 5)
	Salt to taste

Heat the oil and sauté the onion for 1 minute, then add the garlic and sauté 1 minute longer. Add the remaining ingredients and bring the mixture to a boil. Then reduce the heat to a simmer and cook, uncovered, for 30 to 40 minutes, until the mixture starts to thicken up a bit. The mixture can be smoothed out just a little by using a potato masher.

Yield: 2½ cups
Heat Scale: Medium

SANTA FE EXOTIX'S EXCELLENT GREEN CHILE SAUCE

Nobody makes green chile sauce like Todd Sanson. In fact, it's so good that it won an award at the National Fiery Foods Show! Use this sauce on eggs, tofu dishes, beans, enchiladas, and other Southwest specialties. This recipe makes a lot of sauce for the freezer.

4	tablespoons olive or canola oil	¼	cup gold tequila
4	tablespoons minced garlic	2	pints Rich Vegetable Stock (see recipe, p. 5)
5	chopped onions	1	tablespoon salt
3	pounds chopped frozen New Mexican green chile, thawed		

Heat the oil in a small stock pot, sauté the garlic, then add the onions and half of the green chile. Simmer for 10 minutes, add the tequila, and then simmer for another 10 minutes.

Add the remaining green chile, stock, and salt. Simmer all the ingredients for 20 minutes.

Allow the mixture to cool slightly and then puree half of it in a blender or food processor. Return the pureed mixture to the stock pot and stir well. Cool and refrigerate or freeze.

Yield: 8 to 9 cups
Heat Scale: Medium

∿∿∿∿∿∿∿∿∿

CILANTRO AND PIÑON PESTO FOR PASTA

There's nothing like a quick and spicy Southwestern pesto. Substitute basil or Italian parsley for the cilantro to vary the taste. Cook up a pot of your favorite pasta and toss it in this pesto.

1   **cup sour cream**
1   **cup non-fat plain yogurt**
½   **cup piñon nuts, minced**
1   **bunch fresh cilantro**
1   **red jalapeño, seeds and
    stem removed, chopped**

4   **cloves of garlic, peeled**
1   **teaspoon lemon juice**
    Salt and pepper to taste

In a food processor, puree the sour cream, yogurt, and piñons until the nuts are finely minced. Add the cilantro, jalapeño, garlic, lemon juice, and salt and pepper. Puree until smooth.

Yield: 2 cups
Heat Scale: Mild

Onions, the Miracle Drug

Another common ingredient of salsa has many reputed medical applications. Among them are:

- Killing bacteria in the mouth, including those responsible for tooth decay. (It is a remarkable antiseptic.)
- Providing vitamins B and C, plus calcium, iron, potassium, and protein.
- Lowering blood levels of high-density lipoproteins, the molecules that carry cholesterol into the body.
- Curing abscesses on the body or in the mouth.

911 TOMATO-BASIL SAUCE WITH HABANEROS

This blistering tomato sauce will sneak up on you. We suggest you go easy on the habaneros until you've tasted the sauce and figured out which heat level is best. Serve this sauce over your favorite pasta with a salad from Chapter 3.

1	tablespoon olive oil	1	teaspoon habanero powder
2	cloves garlic, crushed		Pinch of sugar
2	scallions, minced	1/3	cup fresh basil, chopped
7	tomatoes, peeled, seeded, and chopped	1/2	stick of margarine, cut into pieces
1/2	cup Rich Vegetable Stock (see recipe, p. 5)		
2	tablespoons tomato paste		

Heat the oil in a large saucepan over low heat. Add the garlic and scallions, then sauté, stirring occasionally, until the scallions are translucent. Add the tomatoes and bring to a boil. Reduce the heat and simmer, uncovered, for about 5 minutes. Add the vegetable stock, tomato paste, habanero powder, and sugar. Stir well and simmer for about 20 minutes or until the mixture becomes thick. After the sauce is thickened, add the basil and whisk in the margarine.

Yield: about 2½ cups
Heat Scale: Hot

〰〰〰〰〰〰

PUNGENT PUTTANESCA SAUCE

The origins of this sauce are obscured in legend and lore, but all the stories are interesting. In Italian, "puttanesca" literally means "harlot's sauce"; this sauce was thought to be a favorite meal of prostitutes because it was nourishing—and quick to make. Another source implies that it was a favorite sauce for married ladies who were having an affair; they would come home late and make this rich sauce, which smelled as if it had been cooking all day. Again, it is to be served over your favorite pasta; or spread it on Italian bread, top it with parmesan cheese, and broil it for a hearty sandwich.

2 **tablespoons olive oil**	2 **tablespoons fresh basil (or 1 tablespoon dried basil)**
2 **garlic cloves, minced**	
¼ **cup onion, minced**	
1 **tablespoon capers, chopped**	3 **tablespoons chopped Italian parsley**
6 **ripe tomatoes, peeled, seeded, and coarsely chopped**	1 **tablespoon crushed red New Mexican chile**
3 **tablespoons tomato paste**	1 **cup Rich Vegetable Stock (see recipe, p. 5)**
½ **cup chopped black olives**	**Salt and pepper to taste**

Heat the oil in a large heavy skillet, then sauté the garlic, onion, and capers for 2 minutes. Add the chopped tomatoes and sauté for 1 minute. Stir in the remaining ingredients, except the stock and salt and pepper, and bring to a boil. Turn the heat to low, add ½ cup of the stock, and stir. Cover and simmer 15 minutes; stir again and add more stock if the mixture starts getting too thick. Simmer, uncovered, for another 15 minutes. The mixture should be slightly thick and chunky.

Yield: About 3 cups
Heat Scale: Mild

〰〰〰〰〰〰

CRANBERRY-HABANERO RELISH

This hot relish is served ice-cold; it creates an interesting palate sensation when the cold relish hits your tongue, followed by the zing of the habanero chiles. It can be served as a relish or as a salad, and it makes an interesting spread on bread. (We have one friend who spreads the relish on bread, tops it off with miniature marshmallows, and broils the sandwich—believe it or not! We haven't tried this combination, and probably won't.) We prefer to use an old-fashioned meat grinder to make the relish because it needs a coarse texture. If you use a blender or a food processor, use the coarsest setting.

1   **16-ounce bag of fresh cranberries, washed and drained**

1   **medium orange, cut into eighths**

¼ **to ½ cup of sugar**

1   **habanero chile, seeds and stem removed (or substitute 2 serrano chiles)**

Lemon or lime juice to taste

Grind the cranberries coarsely, then grind the orange sections into them. Add ¼ cup of the sugar to the mixture and stir. Grind the habanero and add it to the mixture, stirring well. Place the mixture in the refrigerator and let it chill for a few hours. Then taste the mixture; if it is too sweet, add some lemon or lime juice to cut the sugar. If the mixture is too tart for you, add more of the sugar. Then refrigerate until needed.

Serves: 8 as a relish
Heat Scale: Hot

∿∿∿∿∿∿∿∿∿∿∿

HOT AND SOUR SERRANO-CARROT RELISH

This recipe is from Southeast Asia, where hot, sweet, and sour ingredients are commonly combined. Serve this with some grilled vegetables from Chapter 7 and a lemongrass hot rice dish.

2   cucumbers, peeled, halved lengthwise, and seeded

1   tablespoon salt

2/3 cup water

2   tablespoons sugar

1/3 cup distilled white vinegar

1   tablespoon minced bell pepper

1   shallot, minced

1   clove garlic, minced

3   tablespoons chopped cilantro

1   serrano chile, seeds and stem removed, chopped

1/2 cup shredded carrot

2   teaspoons freshly grated ginger

1   teaspoon minced fresh mint

Sprinkle the cucumbers with salt, cover, and refrigerate for 1 hour.

In a small pan, bring the water to a boil, then transfer the water to a bowl. Add the sugar and vinegar and stir until the sugar is completely dissolved. Refrigerate.

Drain the cucumbers and rinse with cold water; rinse again. Pat the cucumbers dry between paper towels and place in a bowl. Add the vinegar mixture, then the remaining ingredients. Mix gently and refrigerate until cool.

Yield: About 2 cups
Heat Scale: Mild

〰〰〰〰〰〰〰〰〰

A GARDENER'S SELECT RELISH

Melissa reports from her garden, "It is certainly not a misstatement to say I probably won't win any gardening awards. But like just about everyone else, I give it a go every summer, and the gardening gods always seem to smile on my herbs. This relish incorporates both mint and basil grown in my garden, along with a sampling of summer melons." Use this to accompany a spicy pasta entree from Chapter 6.

1   orange, peeled and
     diced
1½   cups diced honeydew
     melon
1½   cups diced cantaloupe
½   cup diced red onion
¼   cup chopped fresh basil
1   tablespoon safflower oil
2   tablespoons fresh lime
     juice

1   tablespoon fresh lemon
     juice
1   tablespoon minced fresh
     mint
2   tablespoons grated
     orange peel
1   jalapeño, seeds and stem
     removed, minced
     Salt to taste

Combine all the ingredients in a large bowl and mix well. Let stand at room temperature for at least 1 hour before serving.

Yield: 3 cups
Heat Scale: Mild

Salsa vs. Ketchup

Nineteen ninety-two was a banner year in the fiery-foods industry. For the first time in history, salsa sales exceeded those of ketchup, making salsa the number one condiment sold in the United States. However, ketchup manufacturers have apparently decided that if you can't fight 'em, join 'em—at least four brands of hot and spicy ketchup are now on the market. Incidentally, most people don't realize that the earliest English recipes for ketchup also contained chile peppers and powders.

MADRAS MANGO CHUTNEY

We thank our friend Arthur Pais for this recipe. Arthur, born and raised in Madras, India, knows his region and certainly knows his food. Madras is known for its fiery food and its excellent cuisine, and Arthur says that every home has at least two varieties of chile preserves in the pantry at all times. "Over many front doors hangs a string of green chiles to ward off the evil eye," he wrote in *Chile Pepper* magazine.

This chutney is an excellent accompaniment to curries.

6 serrano chiles, stems and seeds removed, minced	2 tablespoons vegetable oil
6 large green or ripe mangoes, peeled and cut into small pieces	1 tablespoon mustard seeds
	1 teaspoon turmeric powder
1 teaspoon fenugreek seeds	Salt to taste

Using a mortar and pestle, make a paste of the chiles and mangoes. Or coarse-grind them in a food processor.

Crush the fenugreek seeds into a coarse powder and add it to the chile-mango paste.

Heat the oil in a skillet and add the mustard seeds. When they begin to pop, add the paste, turmeric, and salt. Simmer for a few minutes, remove from the heat, and cool.

Yield: 2 to 3 cups
Heat Scale: Hot

ᴧᴧᴧᴧᴧᴧᴧᴧᴧᴧᴧ

DOS CHILES VERDES CHUTNEY

This chutney offers double the pleasure—with both jalapeños and fresh green chile as main ingredients. An equally wonderful benefit is that it has only about 50 calories per serving—so enjoy!

1 cup water
2 cups apple cider vinegar
¾ cup honey
2 cups fresh tomatoes, peeled and chopped
6 tomatillos, husks removed, chopped
1 medium onion, chopped
1 cup golden raisins

½ cup fresh cilantro, chopped
2 green New Mexican chiles, roasted, peeled, seeds and stems removed, chopped
2 jalapeños, seeds and stems removed, chopped
1 teaspoon ground cumin

In a large saucepan, combine all the ingredients, stir, and simmer, uncovered, for 2½ to 3 hours. Remove from heat and cool to room temperature. Serve immediately, or store covered in the refrigerator.

Yield: About 4 cups
Heat Scale: Medium

〜〜〜〜〜〜〜〜〜〜

HOT HORSERADISH MUSTARD

This homemade mustard-horseradish-chile concoction is a perfect condiment for steamed vegetables. Try it over baked potatoes.

½ cup yellow mustard seeds
1 cup dry white wine
½ cup white wine vinegar
2 teaspoons grated fresh horseradish

1 teaspoon sugar
½ teaspoon cayenne powder
1 teaspoon lemon juice

Place the mustard seeds, wine, and vinegar in a medium-sized bowl. Cover and let soak at room temperature for at least 12 hours.

Place the seed mixture in a food processor and blend until creamy—about 2 minutes. Pour this puree into a bowl and add the horseradish, sugar, cayenne, and lemon juice. Mix well until all ingredients are completely blended.

Yield: About 1¼ cups
Heat Scale: Mild

~~~~~~~~~~~~~~~~~~~~~

FENNEL-DILL MUSTARD SAUCE

Here's an accompaniment to steamed vegetables—asparagus, broccoli, or carrots, for example. Or try it as a warm dip for fresh vegetables.

2 cups half-and-half (or 2 cups milk)	2 teaspoons white wine
2 tablespoons fennel seeds	½ teaspoon cayenne powder
3 teaspoons dill	¼ teaspoon salt
6 cloves of garlic, minced	
2 tablespoons Dijon-style mustard	

Combine the half-and-half (or milk), fennel seed, dill, and garlic in a saucepan. Bring to a boil over moderate heat, stirring occasionally. Reduce the heat to low and simmer until the liquid is reduced to about 1 cup. Pour the sauce through a fine strainer into another pan.

Whisk in the mustard, wine, cayenne, and salt. Warm over low heat for about 3 minutes, whisking rapidly. Remove from the heat and place in a serving bowl.

Yield: About 1 cup
Heat Scale: Mild

LIMON TARRAGON MARINADE

This marinade utilizes the citrus tastes of both the lemon and the lime. The tarragon gives the mixture an interesting and tangy taste. Use it to marinate shishkebabs of fresh vegetables and tofu or tempeh before grilling.

1 cup olive oil	2 teaspoons grainy mustard
2 tablespoons fresh lemon juice	2 teaspoons crushed red New Mexican chile
2 tablespoons fresh lime juice	½ teaspoon salt
2 shallots, minced	¼ teaspoon fresh ground pepper
4 teaspoons fresh tarragon, minced	

In a glass bowl, whisk together all the ingredients. Refrigerate for at least 2 hours before using so that the spices can blend.

Yield: 1¼ cup
Heat Scale: Mild

᭧᭧᭧᭧᭧᭧᭧᭧᭧᭧

MEXICAN MAYONNAISE

This mayo is spicy and great as a sandwich spread or as a dip for raw vegetables. Mary Jane suggests you place a dollop alongside some innocent-looking steamed vegetables and see if the guests bite.

2 jalapeño or serrano chiles, seeds and stems removed, chopped	½ teaspoon oregano
	½ teaspoon fresh lime or lemon juice
2 tablespoons fresh cilantro	½ cup low-fat mayonnaise

In a small food processor, puree the chiles, cilantro, oregano, and juice into a paste. Stir the paste into the mayonnaise and chill for an hour. Before using, remove from the refrigerator and let the mixture warm almost to room temperature.

Yield: ½ cup
Heat Scale: Medium

Fiery Foods: Fad or Trend? Part 1

The debate goes on in the media about the longevity of our love for hot and spicy foods. Writing in *The Miami Herald* in 1989, Bob Swift asked, "Will the next hot new food fad be really hot, as in chile peppers? I fear the answer is yes. Food fads come and go. Sushi came and went. So did blackened redfish. Now, I believe, the chile pepper is coming into its own, spreading from the Southwest and Caribbean. Soon, all of us—with the possible exception of devotees of New England boiled dinners—may be burping flames."

All-Natural
Appetizers

They're called *hors d'oeuvres* in France, *antojitos* or *aperitivos* in Latin America, *tapas* in Spain, and *zakuski* in Russia, but they're all the same thing: appetizers. So called in English because they are intended to stimulate the appetite, these delicacies were originally bite-sized morsels served with cocktails before the main meal.

Today, however, their definition has broadened and the word *appetizer* can refer to smaller portions of what normally would be an entree — a little meal before the main meal, if you will. Everything, from pastries to relishes to dips, is now used as an appetizer, and our spicy meatless recipes illustrate the wide variety of foods now being served before the main meal. In fact, in many circles, a collection of appetizers *is* the main meal. They are the ideal entertaining food, and at *Chile Pepper* magazine summer picnics, all of us contribute appetizers such as the ones in this chapter, and then we all have quite a hot and spicy feast.

The spicy, meatless appetizers begin with Disappearing Chile Strips — those basic marinated strips of New Mexican chiles that never stay around very long. Our collection of stuffed peppers comes next, with a recipe from Hungary, Cheese-Stuffed Peppers, that features banana peppers. Our Arizona recipe, Spicy Stuffed Ancho Chiles, is unusual in the fact that these may be the only example of stuffed chiles that are used dried rather than fresh. The fresh version of the ancho, the poblano, is also stuffed in the recipe for Roasted Poblanos Stuffed with Mushroom-Walnut Pesto.

Snacks and dips are the next category of appetizers. Chile-Cumin Crackers are great when spread with low-fat cream cheese, and Peppered Walnuts need no accompaniment. Sweet Potato Chips Dusted with Chimayo Red Chile can be devoured with some of the salsas and condiments from Chapter 1; the Home-Style Fries with Red Chile Salt and Cilantro Ketchup can accompany the grilled vegetables in Chapter 7, as can the Double-Whammy Onion Rings. Two of our favorite dips are New Mexico Pumpkin Seed Dip and Jalapeño Tofu Spread.

Both of our cheese-based appetizers trace their lineage to the American Southwest — and beyond it to Mexico, of course. Chile con Queso Overkill is our favorite version of that dish, based on extensive taste-testing, and Two-Chile Quesadilla Ecstasy is a classic chile appetizer, with our special twist.

Chiles brighten up other vegetables commonly used as appetizers, such as artichokes (Bottoms-Up Artichoke Hearts) and olives (Hot-Shot Olives). Eggplant and other vegetables are combined in our spicy caponata, Chile-Grilled Caponata. Spinach, chiles, and feta cheese flavor Jill's Spanakopitas, and eggplant returns again in Jazzland Caviar, where it is combined with onions and Tabasco sauce.

Topping off our fiery appetizers is a medley of diverse *hors d'oeuvres* of all styles and nationalities: Chile Poppin' Corn Fritters with Serrano Chutney, Hotsy Hummus, Snow Peas Stuffed with Goat Cheese Chipotle Sauce, and Bangkok Nachos.

So, before the meal begins, let the little meal begin!

DISAPPEARING CHILE STRIPS

As the title of this recipe suggests, these marinated chile strips won't last long around a hot and spicy house. They are extremely versatile: They can be rolled up and pegged with a toothpick for an appetizer; they can be used to jazz up a favorite sandwich (we like them with grilled cheese); they can be coarsely chopped and added to your favorite pasta salad; they can also spice up an omelette or a frittata.

1 **pound fresh (or canned) green New Mexican chiles**	¼ **cup red wine vinegar**
¼ **cup olive oil**	1 **clove of garlic, minced**

Roast the chiles, peel them, remove seeds and stems, and cut into ¼-inch-wide strips; or, if using canned whole chiles, rinse them thoroughly, clean out the seeds, cut off the stems, and cut them into ¼-inch-wide strips.

Place the chile strips in a ceramic casserole dish and cover with the remaining ingredients. Stir the mixture very gently to coat the chile. Marinate overnight in the refrigerator.

Yield: 1½ cups
Heat Scale: Mild

CHEESE-STUFFED PEPPERS
(*KOROZOTTEL TOLTOTT PAPRIKA*)

From *Chile Pepper's* European correspondent, Sharon Hudgins, comes these delightful stuffed peppers. She comments, "I first ate these peppers at a Hungarian beer hall in Keszthely on Lake Balaton. In Hungary, the cheese stuffing is often made from Liptói cheese, a soft curd cheese produced from sheep's or goat's milk. The best substitute in the U.S. is a mixture of feta cheese, ricotta cheese, and sour cream." Vary the heat upward by using hot paprika for a garnish. Serve the peppers whole (1 per person for a cold appetizer, or 2 per person for a luncheon main dish).

8	banana peppers, each about 5 inches long (or substitute yellow wax hot)	½	medium onion, finely chopped
1	pound ricotta cheese	¼	cup chives, finely chopped
½	pound feta cheese		Paprika for garnish
2	to 4 tablespoons thick sour cream		

Carefully slice off the top (stem) end of each pepper. Use a small spoon to scoop out the seeds and veins while keeping each pepper pod intact. Wash and dry the peppers and set them in the refrigerator to chill.

Press the ricotta cheese through a sieve into a large bowl. Crumble the feta cheese and press it through the sieve into the same large bowl. Stir until the cheeses are well combined. Stir in the sour cream (using only enough to moisten the mixture slightly), then add the chopped onion and chives. Mix well.

Spoon the mixture into the pepper pods (being careful not to split or tear the pods). Fill each pod completely with cheese. (Use the handle of the larger wooden spoon to press the cheese mixture into all the spaces in the pods.) Place the peppers in a single layer on a large plate, cover loosely with plastic wrap, and refrigerate for at least 2 hours. Just before serving, garnish the exposed cheese (at the end of each pepper) with a sprinkling of paprika.

Yield: 8 stuffed peppers
Heat Scale: Mild

SPICY STUFFED ANCHO CHILES

This recipe is based on one given to us by chef Kurt Zuger of La Hacienda Restaurant at the Scottsdale Princess Resort. Dave and Mary Jane were wined and dined there at a special authors' luncheon, as part of the famous Scottsdale Culinary Festival. Don't let all of the steps intimidate you; the dish is really relatively easy to prepare and the parts can all be made in advance and quickly assembled for serving.

STUFFED CHILES

6	large dried ancho chiles	2	tablespoons fresh lime juice
1	cup cooked beans, black or pinto	1	serrano chile, seeds and stem removed, minced
¼	cup chopped green onions	3	garlic cloves, minced
½	cup minced sun-dried tomatoes	2	tablespoons pure red New Mexican chile powder
½	cup grated manchego cheese	½	teaspoon ground white pepper

Soak the dried ancho chiles in warm water for 20 minutes. Then drain and make a lengthwise slit in each chile. Remove the seeds and the membrane. Toast the chiles for a minute or two in a skillet, then soak them in water for 5 minutes. Drain and dry.

Mix the cooked beans, onions, tomatoes, cheese, lime juice, serrano chile, and spices. Divide the mixture up and stuff into the drained and dried ancho chiles. Warm them in the oven at 200 degrees for 15 minutes.

TOMATO-CARROT SAUCE

6	tomatoes, peeled, seeded, and diced	4	cups of Rich Vegetable Stock (see recipe, p. 5)
4	carrots, peeled and diced		Salt and pepper to taste
1	tablespoon fresh lime juice		

In a large saucepan, sauté the tomatoes and carrots until the carrots are soft. Add the lime juice and the stock and boil rapidly for a minute.

Lower the heat and cook uncovered until the mixture is slightly thickened, stirring occasionally. Let the mixture cool. Add salt and pepper to taste.

CHIPOTLE SAUCE

6 ounces sour cream

1 minced chipotle chile in adobo sauce

1 teaspoon stock

Salt to taste

Mix all of the ingredients together and set aside.

MOLE SAUCE

1 tablespoon red mole (available in Latin markets)

1 tablespoon green mole (available in Latin markets)

1 tablespoon Rich Vegetable Stock (see recipe, p. 5)

Divide the stock between the red and the green mole and mix each thoroughly. Set aside.

TO ASSEMBLE

Pour tomato-carrot sauce onto a small plate, top with the stuffed ancho, top the chile with the chipotle sauce, and drizzle both mole sauces over the top. Serve warm or at room temperature.

Serves: 6 as an appetizer
Heat Scale: Medium

〰〰〰〰〰〰〰

ROASTED POBLANOS STUFFED WITH MUSHROOM-WALNUT PESTO

This appetizer is fairly rich and extremely tasty. The mushroom pesto may also be used as a paté to be served with crackers or chips.

8	medium poblano chiles, roasted, peeled, seeds removed but stems left on	16	fresh medium mushrooms, quartered
4	cups fresh basil leaves	4	cloves garlic
½	cup olive oil	1	teaspoon salt
4	tablespoons piñons or pine nuts	4	ounces low-fat cream cheese, softened
4	tablespoons walnuts, chopped	⅔	cup freshly grated Parmesan cheese

Arrange the poblanos, evenly spaced, on an oiled baking dish and set aside. In a food processor, combine the basil, oil, nuts, mushrooms, garlic, and salt; puree until smooth. Place in a mixing bowl and stir in the cream cheese and Parmesan cheese. Mix well.

Fill the poblanos with the pesto and refrigerate for at least 1 hour. Bake at 400 degrees for 6 to 8 minutes, or until completely heated through.

Serves: 8
Heat Scale: Medium

Snack Guilt

According to *American Demographics* magazine, 9 out of 10 Americans like to snack between meals and 33 percent of those polled feel guilty about it. Snack guilt is greater than the guilt from lying about age (16 percent), not visiting the in-laws regularly (12 percent), and cheating on income taxes (11 percent).

CHILE-CUMIN CRACKERS

These zesty crackers can be served hot or cold; they can even be made two or three days ahead of time and kept in an airtight container. They are good to serve as an appetizer or with a salad for a luncheon.

¾ cup margarine
1 cup shredded sharp cheddar cheese
2 teaspoons New Mexican red chile powder

¼ cup minced onion
1½ teaspoons ground cumin
2 cups sifted all-purpose flour

Cream the margarine and cheese together thoroughly. Add the chile powder, onion, and cumin and mix. Add flour gradually to the cheese-margarine mixture and blend well. Form into rolls about 1½ inches in diameter. Wrap in waxed paper or foil and chill for several hours or overnight. Remove from the paper or foil and, using a chilled, sharp knife, slice each roll thinly (¼ inch) and bake on a lightly greased cookie sheet in a 400-degree oven for about 10 minutes or until lightly browned. Remove from the cookie sheet with a spatula and serve immediately. If not serving immediately, put the crackers on a wire rack to cool thoroughly, and then put them in an airtight container.

Yield: 3 dozen
Heat Scale: Mild

〰〰〰〰〰〰〰

PEPPERED WALNUTS

Hot nuts are quite the rage these days; commercial brands of hot and spicy pistachios, pecans, and peanuts are now available. We add our two cents' worth with the following recipe for walnuts.

1 tablespoon safflower oil	2 teaspoons soy sauce
1 teaspoon freshly ground black pepper	1 teaspoon Tabasco sauce or other Louisiana hot sauce
1 teaspoon cayenne powder	1 teaspoon salt
½ teaspoon dried thyme, crumbled	5 cups shelled and halved walnuts
2 egg whites	

Place a rack in the upper third of the oven and preheat the oven to 375 degrees. Coat a large baking pan with the oil. Mix together the black pepper, cayenne, and thyme in a small bowl.

Mix the egg whites in another bowl until foamy, then whisk in the soy sauce, Tabasco, and salt. Add the nuts and toss to coat. Add the pepper mixture and toss to coat.

Pour the walnuts into the prepared baking pan, spreading evenly. Bake for 4 minutes, stirring the nuts to break up any clumps. Bake until golden brown, watching closely to prevent burning. Baking time is about 10 minutes altogether. Remove from the oven and pour into a bowl. Cool to room temperature before serving.

Yield: 5 cups
Heat Scale: Medium

〜〜〜〜〜〜〜〜

SWEET POTATO CHIPS DUSTED WITH CHIMAYO RED CHILE

This appetizer is a hot twist on party chips. We have had great success substituting sweet potatoes for potatoes, including our version of Spicy Sweet Potatoes Anna (see recipe, p. 179).

Vegetable oil for deep
frying

2 large sweet potatoes,
peeled and cut into
¼-inch wafers

1 tablespoon New Mexican
hot red chile powder
(Chimayo preferred)

Heat the vegetable oil to 350 degrees in a deep skillet. Separate the
potatoes into 6 portions. Fry each batch, turning once, for 1 minute or
until they are golden. With a slotted spoon, transfer the chips to a paper
towel to drain and cool. Continue until all potato chips are fried and
cooled.

Place the red chile powder in a medium-sized plastic bag. Again
working in batches, place the chips in the bag and close it. Shake the
bag gently to dust the chips with the powder. After each batch is dusted,
transfer to a napkin-lined basket and serve.

Serves: 4 to 6
Heat Scale: Medium

∿∿∿∿∿∿∿∿∿

HOME-STYLE FRIES WITH RED CHILE SALT AND CILANTRO KETCHUP

This recipe is the perfect addition to any casual meal, such as grilled
vegetables from Chapter 7. Feel free to add some chile to the ketchup,
or to replace the bland ketchup with one of the habanero or jalapeño
brands on the market.

½ cup ketchup

1 teaspoon cilantro, finely
minced

1 teaspoon balsamic vinegar

2 teaspoons salt

2 teaspoons New Mexican
red chile powder

Vegetable oil for deep
frying

3 large white potatoes,
peeled, dried, and cut
into ¼-inch-thick sticks

In a small bowl, combine the ketchup, cilantro, and vinegar. Mix together the salt and red chile powder in another small bowl. Set both bowls aside.

Place the potato strips on paper towels in a row. Completely cover the strips with the towels and let stand for at least 45 minutes or until potatoes are dry to the touch. Pour the oil into a large skillet and heat to 350 degrees. Separate the potato sticks into 4 equal batches. Fry each batch until just slightly brown. Remove from the oil with a slotted spoon and place on paper towels to drain. Continue until all sticks are done, then cool the fries.

Heat the oil to 400 degrees and fry the sticks again in batches, until they turn a deep golden brown. Using a slotted spoon, transfer the fries to a basket lined with paper towels. Sprinkle the sticks with the red chile salt. Serve with the cilantro ketchup.

Serves: 2 to 4
Heat Scale: Mild

Chiles and Bungees

"But for recreation, many of us enjoy whiling away the evening in the 1990s version of a salon — the new or exotic restaurant. And in those restaurants we communally consume hot peppers: It's politically correct thrill-seeking, in which we can publicly engage — on a date, in a game of I'll show you mine if you show me yours, and with friends or siblings, open challenge without warfare. . . . It's the dining room equivalent of bungee-jumping."
—Jennifer Farley, *Houston Press,* July 23, 1992

DOUBLE-WHAMMY ONION RINGS

Most onion rings from fast-food restaurants feature "re-formed" onions, which are molded back into a ring. Our recipe features actual rings of real onion, and we promise twice the heat with this tasty treat.

⅔ **cup buttermilk**

6 **New Mexican green chiles, roasted, peeled, seeds and stems removed, chopped**

2 **large white onions, cut into ¼-inch-thick rings**

6 **cups vegetable oil for deep frying**

4 **cups all-purpose flour**
Salt to taste
New Mexican hot red chile powder, such as Chimayo

Blend the buttermilk and chiles in a blender until only small bits of chile are still visible to the eye. Pour into a large bowl. Add the onions, completely coating each one. Cover the onion-buttermilk mixture and let stand at room temperature for at least 4 hours, but not more than 5 hours. Preheat the oven to 200 degrees.

Line a baking sheet with enough paper towels to soak up the excess oil after frying. Heat the oil in a deep pan to 325 degrees. Drain the onion rings in a colander, draining off any excess liquid. Thoroughly dredge one fourth of the onion rings in flour. The more flour that sticks, the better!

Fry the onion rings until golden brown, about 3 to 4 minutes. Transfer the onion rings to paper towels on baking sheets, using tongs. Repeat until all rings are fried. Keep rings warm in the oven while completing the other batches. Sprinkle with salt and dust lightly with red chile powder before serving.

Serves: 8
Heat Scale: Medium

NEW MEXICO PUMPKIN SEED DIP

You'll say *oui, oui* to this Parisian party dish, which we have spiced up considerably. Also, here's a great way to use the pumpkin seeds from your garden or from jack-o'-lanterns. Serve the dip with toasted slices of your favorite bread. Feel free to choose a spicy bread from Chapter 8.

1½	cups hulled pumpkin seeds	1	teaspoon salt
3	tablespoons safflower oil	½	teaspoon lemon pepper
1	clove garlic, minced	½	teaspoon New Mexican red chile powder
¾	cup Rich Vegetable Stock (see recipe, p. 5)		
¼	cup lime juice		
2	New Mexican dried red chiles, seeds and stems removed, coarsely chopped		

Preheat the oven to 375 degrees. Place the pumpkin seeds on an ungreased baking sheet. Bake until the seeds are golden brown, stirring occasionally, watching closely to avoid burning. Remove the seeds from the oven and place in a food processor. Puree until finely ground.

In a skillet, heat the oil over moderate heat and sauté the garlic for about 30 seconds. Pour the garlic and oil into the blender with the pureed seeds. Add the stock, lime juice, red chile, salt, and lemon pepper to the blender mixture. Process until the mixture is pureed, stopping to scrape down the sides as needed.

Transfer the dip to a serving bowl and refrigerate. Sprinkle the dip with red chile powder before serving.

Yield: About 1½ cups
Heat Scale: Medium

JALAPEÑO TOFU SPREAD

Soybean meets jalapeño in this interesting cross-cultural blend of flavors. Serve it with the Chile-Cumin Crackers (p. 42).

11	ounces tofu	1½	tablespoons non-fat plain yogurt
½	teaspoon cumin	½	teaspoon dill
½	cup minced red bell pepper	¼	teaspoon dry mustard
¼	cup onions, minced	2	jalapeño chiles, seeds and stems removed, minced
1	tablespoon parsley, chopped		

In a bowl, mash the tofu with a potato masher. Place in a colander and let it drain. When it is drained, return the tofu to the bowl and set aside. In a medium bowl, combine the cumin, bell pepper, onions, parsley, and yogurt. Whisk in the dill, mustard, and jalapeños. Mix well, add the tofu, and continue stirring until the mixture is completely blended.

Yield: About 1 cup
Heat Scale: Medium

〰〰〰〰〰〰〰〰

CHILE CON QUESO OVERKILL

Of all the chile con queso recipes we have tried, this one, created by Mary Jane (revised on the basis of all the previous mistakes she has made), is, in our opinion, by far the best. It is tastiest when served warm and with good-quality tortilla chips. It can also be used as a sauce with baked potatoes, refried beans, freshly cooked vegetables, and grilled vegetables. If you like this dip spicier, add a favorite hot sauce to the recipe.

1 cup Monterey Jack or queso blanco (Mexican white cheese), cubed

½ cup sharp cheddar cheese, cubed

¼ cup light cream or evaporated milk

1 medium tomato, finely chopped

¼ cup chopped New Mexican green chiles, or 1 4-ounce can of chopped chiles, drained and rinsed

2 cloves garlic, minced

2 green onions, finely chopped

In a heavy saucepan or a double boiler, melt the cheeses over low heat. When they are melted, add the cream and stir constantly. Then add the remaining ingredients and stir to mix thoroughly. Add more cream if the mixture looks too thick. Heat and stir for 5 minutes, until it is hot. Serve immediately, or let the mixture cool down a little and refrigerate to serve the next day. The dip really is best if it can be made a day in advance. Bring the mixture back to room temperature, then heat slowly, stirring constantly.

Yield: About 2½ cups
Heat Scale: Mild

〰〰〰〰〰〰

TWO-CHILE QUESADILLA ECSTASY

Trust us — these are not the usual bland quesadillas you have been subjected to in the past. When Mary Jane taught high school in Albuquerque, the cafeteria served basic quesadillas with American cheese and green chile for breakfast. It was good, gooey, and satisfying, but it lacked pizazz — just the kind we've added to these quesadillas. Because of the addition of the sliced jalapeños, this is quite a spicy appetizer. The quesadillas can be served in small wedges as an appetizer, or they can be cut in large slices and served as a main course with a big salad and a luscious dessert.

3	10-inch flour tortillas	1	teaspoon hot sauce (preferably one without a lot of vinegar)
5	green New Mexico chiles, roasted, peeled, seeds and stems removed, chopped (or use 2 4-ounce cans of chopped green chiles, thoroughly drained and rinsed)	¼	cup sliced jalapeño or serrano chiles (fresh if possible)
1½	cups shredded sharp cheddar cheese	10	to 15 button mushrooms, or any other variety, sliced and sautéed slightly in margarine
2	cups shredded queso blanco (Mexican white cheese) or Monterey Jack cheese	¼	cup chopped cilantro Sprigs of cilantro for the garnish
¾	cup sun-dried tomatoes, cut into slivers		

Place one of the tortillas on a small cookie sheet and spread half of the green chiles over the top. Sprinkle half of the cheddar and half of the queso blanco over the chile. Then add half of the sun-dried tomatoes, half of the hot sauce, and half of the jalapeños, mushrooms, and chopped cilantro.

Place the second tortilla over the first one and repeat the process. Then cover with the third tortilla.

Bake in a 400-degree oven for 7 to 9 minutes, until the quesadilla is heated through and the cheese is melted. Slice the quesadilla with a very sharp serrated knife or a very sharp pizza cutter. Serve garnished with the sprigs of fresh cilantro.

Serves: 6
Heat Scale: Hot

BOTTOMS-UP ARTICHOKE HEARTS

Be sure to try this recipe when artichokes are in season. Because arti-chokes tend to be rather bland, the spicy pesto makes a good counter-point. This dish makes an elegant appetizer or first course, and using fresh summer basil gives an intense flavor to the pesto.

½   **cup fresh basil**
1   **clove garlic**
2   **tablespoons grated Romano, Pecorino, or Parmesan cheese**
2   **tablespoons piñons, pine nuts, or walnuts**
2   **teaspoons New Mexican ground red chile**

¼   **cup Chile-Infused Oil (olive preferred; see recipe, p. 6)**
2   **cups curly endive or grilled radicchio**
4   **fresh artichokes, cooked, leaves and choke removed, and cooled**
1   **small tomato, diced**

In a food processor, chop the basil and garlic together. Then add the cheese, nuts, and chile and chop until the nuts are pulverized. Add the oil in a slow stream and keep blending until there is a thick pesto consistency.

Arrange the artichoke hearts (bottoms) on a bed of curly endive or grilled radicchio. Spread the pesto on top of the artichokes and sprinkle with the diced tomato. This dish should be served at room temperature.

Serves: 2
Heat Scale: Mild

〰〰〰〰〰〰〰〰

HOT-SHOT OLIVES

These olives keep for several months in the refrigerator; they can be used as an appetizer or as a spicy addition to salads. Try them chopped and mixed with cream cheese and a little mayo, or as a tangy stuffing for celery or hard-boiled eggs. You can also incorporate them (chopped or sliced) into any dipping recipe to liven it up.

1¼ pounds Kalamata olives

3 garlic cloves, thinly sliced

1½ teaspoons of rosemary, crushed with a mortar and pestle

1 tablespoon New Mexican red chile *molido* or pure red ground chile

2 tablespoons balsamic vinegar

1½ cups olive oil

Drain the olives thoroughly and set aside. Mix the remaining ingredients together and whisk thoroughly.

In a 1-quart jar, place one third of the olives and cover with one third of the whisked mixture; repeat with the next one third of the olives and the mixture, until both are used up.

Allow the olives to stand at room temperature for 24 hours. Then shake the jar well and place it in the refrigerator for two weeks, shaking the jar daily.

Yield: 3 cups of olives
Heat Scale: Mild

〜〜〜〜〜〜〜〜〜

CHILE-GRILLED CAPONATA

This recipe has gone through several incarnations to reach its present delicious state. Rosa Rajkovic, our good friend and executive chef at the Monte Vista Fire Station in Albuquerque, suggested the inclusion of the dill, basil, oregano, and marjoram to add an herbal punch; in addition, she uses fine-quality balsamic vinegar and fresh lemon juice, which we find work well with the smoky, spicy flavor of the grilled eggplant and onions. *Hint:* use a vegetable-grilling screen, so the vegetables don't fall through the wide spaces on the grill. The caponata can be served any number of ways: it can be served on leaves of Bibb lettuce; it can be an antipasto served with toasted baguettes or focaccia bread; or it can be used as a sandwich filling on good rolls.

2½ pounds eggplant, preferably Japanese or white eggplant, peeled and sliced ¾ inch thick	¾ teaspoon dill
	1½ teaspoons basil
	1 teaspoon oregano (Greek or Italian preferred)
2 shallots, peeled and sliced ½ inch thick	
	1 teaspoon marjoram
4 onions, peeled and sliced ½ inch thick	¾ cup green olives without pimento, sliced
¾ cup Chile-Infused Oil (see recipe, p. 6)	½ cup to ¾ cup Kalamata olives, pitted and quartered
1½ pounds Italian plum tomatoes	
⅔ cup balsamic vinegar	2 tablespoons capers, drained
3 tablespoons fresh lemon juice	3 tablespoons piñons or pine nuts
2 teaspoons sugar	

On an outside grill, start a hot fire using a good hardwood, such as oak, pecan, or apple. (Use charcoal only as a last resort.) When the fire is ready, position the rack about 4 to 5 inches from the wood. (If you do not have access to a grill, use the broiler in your oven; just remember that the vegetables will not have the same taste.)

Brush both sides of the eggplant, shallots, and onion with the chile oil. Grill the eggplant 5 to 6 minutes per side, until it is browned and soft inside. Grill the shallots 3 to 4 minutes per side. Grill the onion slices 7 to 8 minutes per side, or until they are slightly charred. Remove the vegetables from the fire and allow them to cool. When they are cool, chop them coarsely and set them aside.

In a large skillet, heat the remaining chile oil (at least 3 tablespoons) and add the tomatoes. Sauté and stir frequently until the tomatoes are slightly thickened, about 10 to 15 minutes. Then add the balsamic vinegar, the lemon juice, the sugar, and the herbs. Cover and simmer slowly for 10 minutes, checking to make sure the mixture doesn't get too dry. (If it starts to dry out, add a little water and remove the mixture from the heat.)

Add the reserved mixture of eggplants, shallots, and onions and mix gently. Then add the olives, capers, and pine nuts and mix again. Chill this mixture for 24 hours.

> Yield: 9 cups
> Heat Scale: Mild

JILL'S SPANAKOPITAS

Our friend Jill Sullivan gave us her recipe for the best version of this Greek appetizer we've had. This is a guaranteed crowd-pleaser — set a few aside for the cook, or they'll disappear before you get a taste.

1 **10-ounce package of frozen leaf spinach, thawed, squeezed dry, and chopped fine**	½ **cup crumbled feta cheese**
4 **scallions with greens, minced**	¼ **pound low-fat cream cheese**
½ **cup minced parsley**	2 **tablespoons grated Parmesan cheese**
⅛ **cup minced jalapeños or serranos**	2 **eggs (or egg substitute)**
½ **teaspoon minced dill**	½ **pound filo dough**
	¼ **pound margarine, melted (or more if needed)**

Preheat the oven to 350 degrees.

In a large bowl, combine the spinach with the scallions, parsley, jalapeños, dill, feta, cream cheese, parmesan, and eggs. Mix until it has a smooth texture, then pour the mixture into a food processor and puree.

Unwrap the filo dough and cover with a slightly dampened towel. Working with 1 filo sheet at a time, brush each sheet with melted margarine and then cut lengthwise into 5 strips. Fold the bottom of the strip over one third of itself. Center ½ teaspoon of mixture on the folded end of the strip (like folding a flag) until you have formed a triangle shape. Repeat until all the spanakopitas are formed.

Arrange the triangles about an inch apart on a greased, foil-lined baking sheet. Brush each triangle with melted margarine and bake for 15 minutes at 350 degrees, or until they are golden brown.

Serves: 8
Heat Scale: Medium

∿∿∿∿∿∿∿∿∿∿

JAZZLAND CAVIAR

This New Orleans favorite can be served on melba toast or any other unsalted crackers. It is also good as a stuffing for celery or tomatoes.

6 small whole eggplants	½ teaspoon salt
6 small red onions, minced	1 cup olive oil
2 cloves garlic, minced	½ cup wine vinegar
1 teaspoon cayenne powder	
2 teaspoons Tabasco sauce (or other Louisiana hot sauce)	

Preheat the oven to 350 degrees. Place the whole eggplants on a baking sheet and bake for about 20 minutes, or until the skins are very dark and wrinkled. Remove from the oven and cool to room temperature. Peel the skins away from the eggplants and drain off any excess liquid. Place the peeled, drained eggplants one at a time in a large bowl and mash with a potato masher until all eggplants are completely mashed. Combine the onions, garlic, and cayenne with the eggplant.

Next, add the Tabasco sauce and salt, mixing well. Finally, add the olive oil and vinegar a little at a time, whisking well after each addition. Chill for at least 1 hour before serving.

Serves: 6 to 8
Heat Scale: Hot

∿∿∿∿∿∿∿∿∿∿∿

CHILE POPPIN' CORN FRITTERS WITH SERRANO CHUTNEY

Serve these tasty fritters for a change of pace; they are convenient to serve because they can be made a little ahead of time along with with the chutney. The slight crunch of the fritter contrasts nicely with the texture of the chopped chutney relish. For a real chile feast, serve these fritters with our Spicy Gazpacho (see recipe, p. 111) for a light lunch entree.

THE FRITTERS

2 cups sifted flour
2 teaspoons baking powder
1 teaspoon sugar
1/4 teaspoon freshly ground black pepper
1 cup low-fat milk
2 egg yolks, lightly beaten (or egg substitute)
2 egg whites, beaten until stiff
2 cups fresh or frozen corn, cooked slightly and cooled
2 tablespoons chopped serrano chiles
1/4 cup finely chopped onion
Vegetable oil for frying

Mix the flour with the baking powder, sugar, and black pepper. Gradually add the milk and the lightly beaten egg yolks to the flour mixture, stirring until the mixture is smooth. Then add the egg whites, corn, chiles, and onion. Gently fold the mixture together until it is well blended.

In a 10- or 12-inch heavy skillet, add ½ inch of vegetable oil and heat until a drop of water will bounce and sizzle on it. Carefully drop heaping tablespoons of the batter into the hot oil; fry until each fritter is golden, then turn it and cook the other side. Drain the fritters on paper towels and keep them warm in a slightly heated oven. Serve immediately when all the fritters are done. Put them on a heated platter and serve the chutney in a bowl surrounded by the hot fritter critters.

Yield: 25 to 30 fritters
Heat Scale: Medium

THE SERRANO CHUTNEY

3   serrano chiles, seeds and stems removed, minced

2   avocados, peeled, seeded, and diced

4   fresh tomatillos, husked and diced

4   scallions, chopped, white part only

1   large or 2 small red tomatoes, coarsely chopped

3   tablespoons chopped fresh cilantro

¼   cup fresh lime juice

Gently mix all of the ingredients together in a ceramic bowl. Allow the mixture to stand at room temperature for 30 minutes before serving. If the mixture is made earlier in the day, refrigerate, then let the chutney reach room temperature before serving.

Yield: 3 cups
Heat Scale: Medium to Hot

HOTSY HUMMUS

This hummus *(houmous)* is a traditional Middle Eastern dish; however, we have added an interesting Southwestern twist — the chipotle chile in adobo sauce, which makes a wonderful, smoky, and spicy dip with lots of bite, rather than just a bland concoction of chickpeas. We have tried numerous chiles and have found that the chipotle chile adds just the right element to bring the hummus out from the bland. Serve it with toasted pita bread quarters or Chile-Cumin Crackers (see recipe, p. 42).

⅓ cup fresh lemon juice

3 tablespoons olive oil or Chile-Infused Oil (see recipe, p. 6)

¼ cup whole sesame seeds

4 cloves garlic, peeled

¼ teaspoon freshly ground black pepper

2 sprigs fresh cilantro

2 cups canned chickpeas, drained and rinsed (or 2 cups of freshly cooked chickpeas)

1 chipotle chile in adobo sauce

In a blender, combine the lemon juice, oil, sesame seeds, garlic, black pepper, and cilantro and blend until the mixture is thick and smooth.

Add one third of the chickpeas and the chipotle chile and process until just smooth. Then add the remaining chickpeas and blend again until just smooth.

Pour the mixture into a serving bowl and refrigerate for at least 2 hours. About ½ hour before serving, remove the bowl from the refrigerator, and let the mixture warm almost to room temperature.

Yield: 2 cups
Heat Scale: Mild

SNOW PEAS STUFFED WITH GOAT CHEESE CHIPOTLE SAUCE

Here is another appetizer using the chipotle chile. This one is attractive and tempting with its smoky-hot, creamy filling.

1 pound snow peas (approximately 40), stems removed

½ cup low-fat cream cheese, softened

½ cup goat cheese, crumbled

2 chipotle chiles in adobo sauce

Rinse and drain the snow peas in a colander. Take each pea pod and slice lengthwise at the seam, creating a pocket. Set aside.

In a food processor, puree the cream cheese, goat cheese, and chipotles. Put the pureed mixture into a pastry bag and use it to fill each snow-pea pocket. Place the filled peas on a platter garnished with greens.

Yield: Approximately 40
Heat Scale: Medium

Fiery Foods: Fad or Trend? Part 2

The *New York Times,* citing the American Spice Trade Association, reports, "The trend toward spicy food continues unabated. Further evidence of the emphasis on prepared foods is the shift in spicy foods from retail to whole-sale. In 1975, 60 percent of spice sales were at the retail level, and now it's only 40 percent."

BANGKOK NACHOS

Ah, nachos, the eternal happy-hour treat! Melissa is happy to report that there is more to this dish than just melted cheese and refried beans. This spicy-sweet dip is also wonderful when served with tortilla strips.

1 **cup plum jelly**	1 **jalapeño chile, seeds and**
½ **cup Madras Mango**	**stem removed, minced**
Chutney (see recipe,	1 **package wonton skins**
p. 30)	**Vegetable oil for deep**
½ **cup balsamic vinegar**	**frying**
1 **teaspoon dried mustard**	

In a large saucepan, combine the jelly, chutney, vinegar, mustard, and jalapeño. Stir over medium heat until the mixture is completely blended and bubbles are visible. Remove from the heat.

Cut wontons in half on the diagonal. Heat the oil to 360 degrees. Fry wontons in batches, until golden brown and blistered. Remove with a slotted spoon and drain on paper towels.

Spoon the sauce into small bowls. Serve at room temperature with wontons on the side for dipping, or sprinkle the sauce over the fried wontons and serve.

Serves: 8

Heat Scale: Medium

Organically Spiced Salads

W e don't believe that a salad should burn out your tastebuds, so we've been quite restrained with the heat levels in this chapter. The salads are generally in the mild to medium range so the heat doesn't overwhelm the herbs and tender greens.

Salads are headed the way of appetizers in regard to their diversity; *Chile Pepper* food editor Nancy Gerlach calls salad "an almost limitless combination of raw vegetables, cooked vegetables, fruits, pastas, and cheese."

We begin this chapter with quite a collection of hot and spicy salad dressings. Santa Fe Serrano Dressing, with avocado, cilantro, and serranos, is great over greens or chilled, cooked vegetables; Spicy Greeny Beany Dressing can be used as a dip with raw vegetables. Fruit salads, if not already spicy, can be charged up with Poppy Seed Dressing, with red chile flakes as the primary incendiary spark. Creamy Jalapeño Dressing, a versatile dressing, is a tasty topping for cooked asparagus; I Can't Believe It's Buttermilk Dressing combines the buttermilk and jalapeños with cucumbers and mustard — perfect for topping exotic greens. Skinny Dipping and Dressing with horseradish and herbs is another great dip for raw vegetables.

Jicama is one of our favorite root crops and combines deliciously with quite a variety of fruits. This crunchy tuber is mild in flavor and is similar in texture to an apple. Our focus on fruits starts with Jicama and Orange Salad, spiced with New Mexican red chile powder. Rujak (Spicy Padang Fruit Salad) is one of the most unusual fruit salads we have ever encountered, featuring a medley of fruits, serrano chiles, and peanuts. Orange Gold Salad features carrots for the orange, tangerines for the gold, and ginger plus chile-infused oil for the heat. Bulgur wheat, pineapples, and nectarines are the foundation for Nectarine-Pineapple Bulgur Salad; habaneros provide the heat.

Our trio of potato salads stars Mary Jane as the top-gun potato salad chef. Over the years, having tested so many different recipes for potato salad, she has reduced her list of hot and spicy ones to three favorites. Red-Hot Potato Salad is flavored with dill, shallots, and serrano chiles. Vegetable Medley Potato Salad features Italian parsley, garlic, and New Mexican chile. Cilantro, hot sauce, and carrots season up our Succulent Southwest Potato Salad.

And what would potato salad be without its complementary cookout fare, cabbage-based coleslaw? Spicy Sweet and Sour Coleslaw is zapped by serranos; Zippy Apple Coleslaw is zipped with a combination of poblanos and chipotles.

Our next four salads feature breads and black-eyed peas. Green Chile Panzanella (Southwest-Style Tuscan Bread Salad) is like tossing Florence and Santa Fe in the same bowl; Zesty French Bread Salad melds the flavors of red onions, cucumbers, basil, and serrano chiles. The good-luck black-eyed peas are represented by Lucky Southwest Caviar (featuring serranos again) and by Curried Good Luck Fruit Salad, in which curry gives an exotic flavor to apples, pineapple, and onion.

We've collected an interesting bunch of salads to finish this chapter, including Spicy Cold Cucumber Salad, with mint, yogurt, and red chile powder. Chilly Chile Lentil Salad combines that little legume with balsamic vinegar, piñons, and habaneros; Brown Rice and Snow Pea Salad with Rojo Vinaigrette is a tempting blending of cooked rice with snow peas, corn, and jalapeños topped with a vinegar–cayenne–brown sugar dressing. Spinach is the star of Popeye's Favorite Goes Fresh and

Spicy (with jicama, mangoes, avocados, and red chile powder). Our final salad, Recycled Salad, is so named because it is made by tossing leftover bell peppers and scallions together with black beans, tomatoes, and poblano chiles.

And remember, if you are serving one of these salads with bland foods, feel free to increase its heat level by adding more of the specified chile.

Great Moments in American Salads

1796: The earliest known American cookbook, Amelia Simmons' *American Cookery,* mentions several different varieties of lettuce. It is commonly believed that American colonists did not have salads, but that is a myth. A rich variety of greens was available in the colonies and Thomas Jefferson mentioned that lettuce, tomatoes, cress, endive, cabbage, tomatoes, parsley, radishes, and cucumbers were available in markets to make salads.

March 1893: At the opening of the Waldorf Hotel in New York, chef Oscar Tschirky creates the Waldorf salad, which is composed simply of apples, celery, walnuts, and mayonnaise. It led the way for the establishment of fruit salads in this country.

July 4, 1924: The Caesar salad is invented in Tijuana, Mexico, by restaurateur Alex Cardini, who names the salad after his brother, Caesar. Caesar's Hotel in Tijuana still serves the salad, which is also still popular in restaurants across the United States.

SANTA FE SERRANO DRESSING

It is necessary to make this dressing in small batches because the avocado will discolor slightly on the second day; however, it is so good and so versatile that it probably won't last that long anyway. We have found that using champagne vinegar adds zest without the harshness associated with other types of vinegars. For a tasty and unusual touch, serve the dressing over cooked chilled vegetables, such as fresh asparagus or artichokes.

1   ripe avocado, peeled, seed removed, and cut into quarters
2   tablespoons champagne vinegar
¼   cup water
½   cup unflavored low-fat yogurt or sour cream

2   tablespoons cilantro
¼   teaspoon salt
1   teaspoon sugar
1   clove garlic
1   fresh serrano chile, seeds and stem removed

Place all the ingredients in a blender or food processor and blend until thoroughly mixed. If the dressing seems too thick, add more water or yogurt. Use as soon as possible; store, covered tightly, in the refrigerator until ready to use.

Yield: 1½ cups
Heat Scale: Mild

~~~~~~~~~~~~~~~~~

SPICY GREENY BEANY DRESSING

This dressing can be used over greens, as a potato salad dressing, and as a dip for fresh vegetables. The spiciness is offset by the cheese-and-yogurt infusion, and the overall flavor is a trip for the tastebuds.

1 **cup low-fat, small-curd cottage cheese**
¼ **cup plain yogurt**
2 **tablespoons milk**
1 **cup green beans, cooked and drained**
½ **cup grated sharp cheddar cheese**
2 **tablespoons champagne vinegar or white wine vinegar**

¼ **teaspoon salt**
¼ **teaspoon freshly ground black pepper**
1 **teaspoon bottled hot pepper sauce (Caribbean preferred)**
¼ **cup chopped onion**
2 **tablespoons horseradish**

Place the cottage cheese, yogurt, and milk in a blender; cover and process until the mixture is smooth. Add one half of the cooked green beans and the remaining ingredients; blend until smooth. Add the remaining green beans and blend until the beans are just finely chopped.

Yield: 1½ cups
Heat Scale: Mild

∿∿∿∿∿∿∿∿∿∿∿

POPPY SEED DRESSING

This makes an unusual dressing for fruit salad because of the spice of the dry mustard and the red chile flakes. It can even be used for basting during the last 2 or 3 minutes of grilling vegetables; because of its sugar content, you don't want to use it too soon, or the vegetables will burn.

½   cup sugar
1½ teaspoons dry mustard
½   teaspoon salt
¼   teaspoon celery salt
1   teaspoon hot red chile
    flakes (such as piquin)

½   teaspoon paprika
⅓   cup cider vinegar
1½ tablespoons poppy seeds
1   cup vegetable oil

Combine all the ingredients in a small bowl and beat with a small electric beater until the salad dressing is thick. Refrigerate.

Yield: About 1½ cups
Heat Scale: Medium

〰〰〰〰〰〰

CREAMY JALAPEÑO DRESSING

The use of watercress gives this dressing peppery overtones, and the jalapeños are what really gives it some zing. It is good served over salad greens, as well as poured over tender-crisp cooked vegetables such as asparagus. You might even like it as a dip for carrots, jicama, turnip spears, and celery.

1   small bunch parsley,
    washed and drained
1   bunch watercress,
    washed and drained
½   cup canola oil
½   cup olive oil
1   clove garlic
⅓   cup tarragon vinegar

2   jalapeño or serrano
    chiles, seeds and stems
    removed
2   shallots, cut into quarters
2   teaspoons dry mustard
1   tablespoon horseradish
1   teaspoon soy sauce
¼   cup plain yogurt

Combine all the ingredients in a food processor or blender and puree. If the mixture seems too thick, add a few teaspoons of yogurt or ice water.

Yield: 2 cups
Heat Scale: Medium

∿∿∿∿∿∿∿∿∿∿

I CAN'T BELIEVE IT'S
BUTTERMILK DRESSING

This low-fat dressing should help get you over the fat hump, and besides, buttermilk is good for you. For an unusual salad, grill some red bell peppers, peel them, cut them in wide strips, chill, and top with this dressing.

1 cup buttermilk
2 red jalapeño chiles, seeds and stems removed, minced
1/3 cup grated cucumber
3 scallions, chopped (with a little tender green included)
1 tablespoon Dijon-style mustard

2 tablespoons fresh cilantro, chopped
2 teaspoons fresh lime juice
1/2 teaspoon dill
1/8 teaspoon freshly ground black pepper

Place all the ingredients in a large glass jar and shake briskly. Chill the dressing and shake again before using.

Yield: 1¼ cups
Heat Scale: Medium

SKINNY DIPPING AND DRESSING

Dip your raw veggies in (or dress up your favorite salad with) this low-fat dressing with a highly enjoyable taste. Try it over mixed greens or sliced tomatoes and avocados.

½ **cup plain non-fat yogurt**

½ **cup lite mayonnaise (Weight Watchers works well)**

1 **tablespoon horseradish, drained**

2 **serrano or jalapeño chiles, seeds and stems removed, ground**

1 **tablespoon Dijon-style mustard**

1 **tablespoon fresh parsley, chopped**

1 **teaspoon fresh tarragon, minced**

¼ **cup low-fat buttermilk**

Combine the yogurt, mayonnaise, horseradish, chile, mustard, parsley, and tarragon. Mix well. Using a whisk, gradually pour the buttermilk into the dressing. Add more or less buttermilk to control the consistency.

Yield: About 1½ cups
Heat Scale: Medium

〰〰〰〰〰〰〰

JICAMA AND ORANGE SALAD

Jicama is a Mexican root vegetable; its taste and consistency are a combination of water chestnut, apple, and potato. In fact, some cooks substitute jicama for water chestnuts in Asian recipes. It can be combined with any number of fruits and vegetables because it blends so well with so many flavors.

1   **head romaine lettuce, cleaned and dried**

¹⁄₂ **pound jicama, peeled and sliced paper-thin**

6   **seedless oranges, peeled and sectioned**

2   **red onions, sliced**

2   **teaspoons ground New Mexican red chile powder**

¹⁄₂ **cup olive oil**

6   **tablespoons fresh lime juice**

3   **tablespoons red wine vinegar**

3   **tablespoons orange marmalade**

   Freshly ground black pepper

Line a shallow bowl with the romaine leaves. Alternate overlapping circles of jicama, oranges, and onion rings on the leaves.

    Combine the remaining ingredients in a small glass jar and shake well. Pour the dressing over the salad and serve immediately.

Serves: 4 to 6
Heat Scale: Medium

〜〜〜〜〜〜〜〜〜

RUJAK
(SPICY PADANG FRUIT SALAD)

World traveler Jeff Corydon, who provided this recipe in an article for *Chile Pepper*, says that the secret of this spicy salad is in the sauce, and that the local taste is honored by including crushed peanuts and additional chiles. Any firm fleshy fruit can be used, such as underripe bananas, carambolas, Asian pears, and even some vegetables such as jicama or cucumber.

1	quart water	4	serrano chiles, seeds and stems removed
1	teaspoon salt		
1	pomelo or tart pink grapefruit, sectioned	2	tablespoons dried tamarind pulp
2	mangoes, slightly under-ripe, peeled, and cut into bite-size pieces	2	tablespoons hot water
		¼	cup palm sugar or dark brown sugar
2	tart apples, peeled and cut into bite-size pieces	1	cup water
		½	cup unsalted, roasted crushed peanuts (or ¼ cup crunchy peanut butter)
1	small pineapple, peeled and cut into bite-size pieces		

Mix the water with the salt and add the pomelo or grapefruit, mangoes, apples, and pineapple and soak overnight in the refrigerator.

Place the chiles in a blender and process until smooth.

Make tamarind water by mashing the dried tamarind in the 2 tablespoons of hot water until it softens and dissolves. Strain the mixture to remove any seeds or tissue.

Melt the brown sugar in a pan with 1 cup of water over low heat until the sugar dissolves, about 5 minutes. Add the crushed peanuts, the processed chiles, and the tamarind water, and simmer for 5 minutes, stirring often, until a fairly thick, sticky syrup forms. Put the syrup in the refrigerator to chill.

When ready to serve, drain the water from the fruits. Pour the syrup over the fruits and toss to coat evenly. Serve at once.

Serves: 8

Heat Scale: Medium

ORANGE GOLD SALAD

We love freshly grated ginger, but sometimes the stringiness involved in preparing it clogs up the mini-processor and drives us crazy. However, a suggestion from a fine Vietnamese chef, Binh Duong, has solved the problem. Binh suggests placing the whole pieces of ginger over a high electric burner or a low gas burner, and turning them every minute or so to char the ginger on all sides. Then rinse the charred ginger under water while scrubbing with a stiff vegetable brush. The ginger is then ready for chopping, grating, or processing. This salad can be served on Boston (Bibb) lettuce leaves or curly endive.

1 cup coarsely grated carrot	2 tablespoons finely chopped fresh ginger
2 oranges or 3 tangerines, peeled and sliced into thin rounds	3 tablespoons rice vinegar
¼ cup finely chopped shallots	2 tablespoons Chile-Infused Oil (olive preferred; see recipe, p. 6)
½ teaspoon basil	¼ teaspoon freshly ground white pepper

In a medium glass bowl, toss the first three ingredients. Then mix the remaining ingredients in a glass jar and shake thoroughly. Pour the dressing over the carrot mixture and toss gently. Chill for 1 or 2 hours before serving.

Serves: 3 to 4
Heat Scale: Mild

NECTARINE-PINEAPPLE BULGUR SALAD

The secret of this salad is its chill. Make sure you refrigerate it for at least 1 hour before serving.

2 **cups bulgur wheat**	⅔ **cup olive oil**
6 **cups boiling hot water**	¼ **cup dill, minced**
2 **cups fresh pineapple, cut into ½-inch pieces**	4 **scallions, chopped**
2 **ripe medium nectarines, peeled, seeded, and cut into ½-inch pieces**	½ **habanero chile, seeds and stem removed, minced** **Nectarine slices for garnish**
¼ **cup fresh lime juice**	

Soak the bulgur in the hot water, removed from the heat, for 30 minutes. Drain thoroughly and transfer to a large bowl. Add the remaining ingredients except the nectarine slices and stir to combine. Refrigerate for at least 1 hour. Add nectarine garnish and serve.

Serves: 8
Heat Scale: Medium

〰〰〰〰〰〰〰〰〰〰

RED HOT POTATO SALAD

This simple potato salad is served warm and can be put together quickly after the potatoes are boiled. The recipe can be doubled or tripled easily. It's a nice change from the ordinary potato salad, and the flavors will really charge your palate.

10 small red potatoes,
  scrubbed thoroughly,
  skins left on

¼ cup rice wine vinegar or
  champagne vinegar

¼ cup Chile-Infused Oil
  (olive preferred; see
  recipe, p. 6)

2 tablespoons fresh dill or
  1 tablespoon dried dill

¾ cup chopped shallots

2 serrano or jalapeño
  chiles, stems removed,
  sliced into thin rings
  Salt and pepper to taste

Place the potatoes in a large Dutch-style oven and cover with water. Bring the pot to a boil and then turn it down to a low boil. Cook the potatoes, uncovered, for 10 to 15 minutes, testing them by inserting a sharp knife through the center of the potato. The potatoes should just start to yield to the knife. Do not overcook. Drain the potatoes and place them in a large bowl.

Using a sharp knife, cut the potatoes into halves (if they are small) or quarters (if they are large). Sprinkle the vinegar over the tops of the potatoes and then sprinkle them with the chile oil. Toss gently. Add the dill, the shallots, the pepper rings, and the salt and pepper; toss gently. Serve warm.

Serves: 3 to 4
Heat Scale: Medium

~~~~~~~~~~~~~~~~

VEGETABLE MEDLEY POTATO SALAD

Here are a few recommendations to make this salad as tasty as possible. First, buy good white wine vinegar. Second, make sure you use Italian parsley for its spark, and if you can't find it, grow it, or substitute watercress with its peppery overtones. And third, be prepared to run out of salad — it really is that good.

4   large russet potatoes
¼   cup white wine vinegar
1   clove garlic, minced
¾   cup chopped green
    onions
1   cup celery, diced
2   hard-boiled eggs — chop
    the whites only (feed the
    yolks to the dog)
¼   cup chopped Italian
    parsley
⅔   cup cucumber, peeled,
    seeded, and diced

½   cup chopped New Mexi-
    can green chile
¾   cup low-fat mayonnaise
¼   cup plain yogurt
1   tablespoon horseradish
2   tablespoons Dijon-style
    mustard
½   teaspoon salt
¼   teaspoon freshly ground
    black pepper

Place the potatoes in a large Dutch oven and cover with water. Bring the water to a boil, and turn the heat down so that the water is at a gentle boil. Cook for 15 to 20 minutes. Do not overcook, or you will have mashed potato salad! Drain the potatoes — they still need to be hot. Pierce each potato with a fork and peel quickly. On a cutting board, slice the potatoes lengthwise and then slice into ¼-inch-thick slices and put them into a large bowl. Sprinkle the slices with the vinegar.

Add the garlic, green onion, celery, chopped whites of the hard-boiled eggs, parsley, cucumber, and chile to the potatoes and toss gently.

In a small bowl, whisk the mayonnaise, yogurt, horseradish, mustard, salt, and black pepper together. Pour this mixture over the potato-vegetable mixture and toss gently to coat. Serve slightly chilled.

Serves: 6
Heat Scale: Mild

SUCCULENT SOUTHWEST POTATO SALAD

Here is the third in our trio of potato salads. It calls for chile powder and sauce instead of pods to elevate the heat level.

4 medium russet potatoes	1 8-ounce can whole-kernel corn, drained and rinsed
¼ cup olive oil	
¼ cup white wine vinegar	
2½ teaspoons red New Mexican chile powder	½ cup coarsely shredded carrot
1 teaspoon bottled hot sauce (we prefer Uno hot sauce)	⅓ cup chopped green bell pepper
½ cup chopped onion	½ cup sliced ripe olives

Place the potatoes in a large Dutch-style oven and cover with water. Bring the water to a boil, then turn the heat down so that the water is at a gentle boil. Cook the potatoes for 15 to 20 minutes or until a knife pierces them easily. Drain, peel, and cube the potatoes; put them into a large bowl while still warm.

In a small glass jar, combine the oil, vinegar, chile powder, and hot sauce and shake vigorously. Pour over the potatoes and toss gently. Add the remaining ingredients and toss gently.

Refrigerate for 1 hour before serving.

Serves: 4 to 6
Heat Scale: Medium

SPICY SWEET AND SOUR COLESLAW

This excellent slaw is a far cry from the mayonnaise-heavy ones of childhood picnics. Because there is no mayo in this one, it is an excellent choice for a modern-day picnic or an outdoor barbecue. The leftovers are great and will keep for five days.

3	pounds fresh green cabbage, thinly sliced	1½	cups chopped onion
¼	cup chopped serrano chiles	1	cup vegetable oil
1	green bell pepper, finely chopped	1	cup white vinegar
1	red bell pepper, finely chopped	1½	cups sugar
		2	tablespoons celery seed
		½	teaspoon freshly ground black pepper

In a very large glass bowl, combine the cabbage, serranos, bell peppers, and onion.

Combine the remaining ingredients in a saucepan and bring to a boil, stirring until the sugar dissolves. Boil gently for 1 minute, then pour the marinade over the vegetables and mix.

Refrigerate for several hours before serving; overnight is the best.

Before serving, drain the slaw so that the marinade doesn't drown everything else on the plate. Save the marinade to add to any leftover slaw.

Serves: 10 to 12
Heat Scale: Medium

ZIPPY APPLE COLESLAW

A little Chimayo red chile makes our second version of hot and spicy coleslaw a memorable salad at any summer picnic.

1 small red cabbage, shredded	1 chipotle chile in adobo sauce, pureed
3 apples, peeled, cored, and shredded	½ cup lemon juice
2 cups diced red bell pepper	½ cup plain non-fat yogurt
2 cups diced red onion	½ cup light mayonnaise
3 poblanos, roasted, peeled, seeds and stems removed, diced	Dash of salt
	1 tablespoon New Mexican hot red chile powder (Chimayo preferred)

Combine the shredded cabbage, apples, bell pepper, red onion, and poblanos in a large bowl. Set aside.

In a large bowl, mix the pureed chipotle and the lemon juice. Next add the yogurt, mayonnaise, salt, and red chile powder. Mix well. Pour the dressing over the cabbage, apple, and pepper cole slaw. Toss to coat evenly. Refrigerate for at least 2 hours before serving.

Serves: 10 to 12
Heat Scale: Medium

〜〜〜〜〜〜〜

GREEN CHILE PANZANELLA (SOUTHWEST-STYLE TUSCAN BREAD SALAD)

In this recipe, it is very important to use red wine vinegar and olive oil of the very best quality, because even the heat of the green chile will not mask the biting taste of inferior products. This salad is surprisingly refreshing on a hot day because of the vinegar and the fresh vegetables.

This is also a great way to use up leftover bread — but once again, it has to be bread with substance. Soft, squishy, store-bought, plastic-wrapped bread will make a salad akin to Elmer's Glue!

10 **slices of good-quality coarse-grained bread, several days old**	2 **cloves garlic, minced very fine**
Water to soak the bread	1 **cup chopped New Mexican green chile**
3 **very fresh tomatoes, peeled and coarsely chopped**	½ **cup fresh basil, chopped**
	¼ **cup red wine vinegar**
2 **cucumbers, peeled, seeded, and cubed**	¼ **teaspoon salt**
	¼ **teaspoon freshly ground black pepper**
1 **cup finely diced red onion**	⅔ **cup best olive oil**

In a large bowl, soak the bread with a little water, but don't get the bread totally soggy. Squeeze the bread dry with your hands and crumble it into a large bowl. Add the tomatoes, cucumbers, red onion, garlic, chile, and basil and toss with the bread.

Pour the vinegar into a small glass jar and add the salt and black pepper. Shake the jar until the salt is dissolved. Then add the olive oil to the jar and shake again until the mixture is blended. Immediately pour the vinegar-and-oil mixture over the bread mixture and toss gently. Serve immediately.

Serves: 6
Heat Scale: Medium

ZESTY FRENCH BREAD SALAD

Here's another bread salad to make with crusty French or Italian bread that's hard enough to put your eye out! Choose the texture of the salad by choosing the amount of time you allow it to sit. For a crunchy salad, serve it immediately. The longer it sits, the softer the salad will become as it soaks up the dressing and vegetable juices.

3   cups of stale, crusty French bread, lightly toasted and cubed in ½-inch pieces

½   cup red onion, finely chopped

1   cucumber, peeled, quartered lengthwise, and cut crosswise into ½-inch pieces

2   large tomatoes, peeled, seeded, and chopped

1   cup basil leaves, firmly packed

1   garlic clove, minced

2   serrano chiles, stems removed

¼   cup red wine vinegar

½   cup olive oil

In a large bowl, combine the bread, red onion, cucumber, and tomatoes. Toss the mixture well. In a food processor, blend the basil, garlic, chiles, vinegar, and olive oil until the basil is pureed and the dressing is emulsified. Sprinkle the dressing over the bread mixture, tossing it well. Serve at once or allow to sit for a few minutes and soften. Serve at room temperature.

Serves: 4
Heat Scale: Medium

〰〰〰〰〰〰〰〰〰

LUCKY SOUTHWEST CAVIAR

Our friends from the South tell us that they always eat black-eyed peas on New Year's Eve and on New Year's Day to ensure good luck for the coming year. We liked that tradition, so we came up with a hot and spicy version of the traditional cooked peas. Serve these in lettuce cups at your next New Year's buffet — for good luck and good health.

4   **cups freshly cooked black-eyed peas (or 2 16-ounce cans), drained, rinsed, and chilled**

½   **cup olive oil**

¼   **cup red wine vinegar (or champagne vinegar for less of a bite)**

1   **tablespoon balsamic vinegar**

½   **teaspoon freshly ground black pepper**

1   **clove garlic, minced**

½   **cup diced celery**

½   **cup chopped onion**

½   **cup chopped green bell pepper**

3   **serrano chiles, seeds and stems removed, minced**

Combine all the ingredients in a large glass bowl and stir to coat thoroughly. Cover and place the bowl in the refrigerator so the mixture can marinate for 2 to 6 hours.

Serve in lettuce cups or on a bed of shredded lettuce. Garnish with radish rosettes, if desired.

Serves: 8 to 10
Heat Scale: Medium

CURRIED GOOD LUCK FRUIT SALAD

Another lucky dish to start the New Year out right, this slightly curried combination of peas and fruits is also mustard- and vinegar-infused! What a combination! This recipe is designed to serve at a picnic or a family get-together.

4 **15-ounce cans black-eyed peas, rinsed and well drained**	½ **cup yogurt**
2 **cups diced apples**	3 **tablespoons Dijon-style mustard**
2 **cups diced fresh pineapple**	2 **tablespoons cider vinegar**
1 **small red onion, minced**	½ **cup olive oil**
2 **tablespoons curry powder**	2 **large purple cabbages**

Combine the black-eyed peas, apples, pineapple, and onion in a large bowl and set aside.

Whisk the curry powder, yogurt, mustard, and vinegar together. Gradually whisk in the olive oil. Refrigerate for at least 4 hours to ensure that the flavors are blended.

Add the dressing to the salad, and gently toss to coat. Peel whole leaves off the purple cabbage to line one large bowl or twelve separate salad bowls. Fill with the fruit salad and serve.

Serves: 12
Heat Scale: Mild

〰〰〰〰〰〰〰

SPICY COLD CUCUMBER SALAD

This salad has a bite, but the yogurt cools it down nicely. We like to make it in the summer when we can get the majority of the ingredients from the garden; sometimes cucumbers from the grocery store can be a little bitter. Taste the cucumber; if it seems bitter, slice it, put it in a colander, and salt it. Let it stand for 30 minutes, rinse thoroughly to remove the salt, and allow to drain.

2   cucumbers, peeled and
    coarsely chopped
1   tomato, finely chopped
3   scallions, finely chopped,
    including some of the
    green
½   teaspoon cumin
2   tablespoons finely
    chopped fresh mint (or
    1 tablespoon dried mint)

1   clove garlic, minced
1   teaspoon New Mexican
    red chile powder
½   to ¾ cup plain low-fat
    yogurt
    Dash sugar (optional)
    Salt and black pepper to
    taste

Combine the first seven ingredients and mix gently. Spoon ½ cup of yogurt over the top and mix again. If the yogurt doesn't cover all of the vegetables, add ¼ cup more. If it seems too sharp, add a dash of sugar; then add the salt and pepper to taste.

Chill for 2 hours or more.

Serves: 4
Heat Scale: Mild

Two Hot Quotes

"[I like the] excitement . . . the raw adrenal energy . . . a kind of hormonal buzz."
— James Beard Award winner Robert Del Grande, July 1992.

"What chiles all have in common is a pungency that is habit-forming and without which food is insipid and without character."
— Copeland Marks, author of *The Exotic Kitchens of Indonesia*

CHILLY CHILE LENTIL SALAD

Lentils have been given short shrift by many people, but they are extremely versatile, nutritious, and cheap, cheap! In this spicy salad/entree, a variety of textures adds interest to the dish, along with the variety of flavors. Our preferred pepper for this dish is the habanero; it delivers a pungent punch.

1 **pound dried lentils, cleaned and washed**	½ **cup cooked, chilled wild rice**
Water to cover	2 **cups cherry tomatoes, halved**
1 **whole onion, peeled**	
6 **whole cloves**	⅔ **cup toasted piñons or pine nuts**
2 **carrots, each cut into 4 pieces**	¼ **to ½ cup chopped fresh cilantro, to taste**
2 **teaspoons chopped fresh oregano (or 1 teaspoon dried oregano)**	½ **cup crumbled feta cheese**
	½ **cup sliced scallions**
2 **cloves garlic, minced**	1 **habanero chile, seeds and stem removed, minced (or substitute 3 red serranos)**
1 **whole bay leaf**	
⅓ **cup balsamic vinegar**	
½ **cup olive oil**	

In a large, heavy saucepan, cover the lentils with water. Add the onion, stuck with the 6 cloves, and the carrots, the oregano, the garlic, and the bay leaf. Bring to a boil, then lower the heat to a simmer and cover. Simmer for 25 to 35 minutes, or until the lentils are done but still retain their shape and are not mushy. Drain thoroughly and discard the carrots, the onion with the cloves, and the bay leaf.

Carefully put the cooked lentils in a large mixing bowl.

Whisk the vinegar and olive oil together. Pour over the lentils and toss gently. Chill for 1 hour or longer.

Then add the remaining ingredients and gently toss to distribute all the ingredients. Cover and chill until ready to serve.

Serve on a bed of chilled greens; use something interesting such as rocket or radicchio. Or use curly endive, watercress, or Bibb lettuce.

Add Chile-Cumin Crackers (p. 42) for a final touch, or one of the warm spoonbreads from Chapter 8.

Serves: 8 as an entree or 12 as a first-course salad
Heat Scale: Medium to Hot, depending on the habanero

^^^^^^^^^^^^^^^^^

BROWN RICE AND SNOW PEA SALAD WITH ROJO VINAIGRETTE

Brown rice adds an interesting flair to this easy-to-make-and-serve salad. The heat is dependent on jalapeños, but feel free to change to any fresh hot chile you happen to find in your garden.

3½ **cups cooked long-grain brown rice**	2 **tablespoons fresh lime juice**
2 **cups fresh snow peas, rinsed**	1 **tablespoon red wine vinegar**
1½ **cups cooked fresh corn kernels**	1 **tablespoon brown sugar, packed**
⅓ **cup scallions, chopped**	1 **teaspoon cayenne powder**
2 **jalapeño chiles, seeds and stems removed, minced**	1 **teaspoon salt**
⅓ **cup corn oil**	½ **teaspoon ground cumin**

Cool the cooked rice for at least 1 hour. While waiting for the rice to cool, combine the snow peas, corn, scallions, and jalapeños. Toss lightly.

In a small bowl, whisk together the corn oil, lime juice, vinegar, brown sugar, cayenne, salt, and cumin. Mix until the sugar is dissolved and the vinaigrette is well blended.

Combine the cooled rice with the snow-pea mixture. Sprinkle the dressing over the salad. Toss to coat the ingredients evenly. The salad should stand at room temperature for at least 1 hour before serving. It can be refreigerated for up to two days, covered.

Serves: 6 to 8
Heat Scale: Medium

∿∿∿∿∿∿∿∿∿∿∿∿

POPEYE'S FAVORITE GOES FRESH AND SPICY

Popeye would have kicked his canned-spinach habit for this fruity, hot, fresh spinach salad.

2   **bunches spinach leaves, washed, dried, stems removed, torn into bite-size pieces**

1   **cup fresh jicama, julienne-cut**

1   **mango, peeled, seeded, and cut into crescents (be sure to find one that is not overly ripe)**

2   **ripe avocados, peeled, seeded, and cut into crescents**

2   **tablespoons fresh lime juice**

1   **tablespoon fresh lemon juice**

½   **teaspoon ground cumin**

1   **teaspoon New Mexican red chile powder (Chimayo preferred)**

½   **teaspoon salt**

⅓   **cup vegetable oil**

Place the spinach in a large salad bowl. Sprinkle the jicama, mango, and avocados over the spinach. Set aside.

   In a bowl, whisk together the lime juice, lemon juice, cumin, chile powder, and salt. Drizzle in the oil, whisking the dressing until it is emulsified. Whisk the dressing one more time before adding it to the salad.

Serves: 8
Heat Scale: Mild

RECYCLED SALAD

We don't know about everyone, but we always seem to buy one too many bell peppers and scallions at the store. Scare up a few black beans, and you'll be able to give some of the orphans in your refrigerator a second try with this textured, tasty salad.

1   **16-ounce can black beans, rinsed and drained**

1   **red or green bell pepper (whichever you have on hand) seeds and stem removed, diced**

½   **cup fresh tomatoes, seeded and diced**

2   **scallions, sliced**

2   **poblano chiles, roasted, peeled, seeds and stems removed, chopped**

1   **tablespoon chopped cilantro**

1   **tablespoon corn oil**

1   **tablespoon fresh lime juice**

¼   **teaspoon salt**

⅛   **teaspoon freshly ground black pepper**

Place the beans in a bowl. Add the bell pepper, tomatoes, scallions, poblanos, and cilantro. Toss well.

In another bowl, whisk the corn oil, lime juice, salt, and pepper together. Drizzle the dressing over the bean salad, and toss gently to coat.

Serves: 4
Heat Scale: Mild

Super, Hot Soups
and Stews

W e love soups and stews, especially in the winter. Like bread, they take quite a while to make, and their fragrance fills the kitchen and soon spreads throughout the house. They are usually thought of as "comfort foods," those tried-and-true favorites that will never let you down.

"While a bowl of vegetables is just a bowl of vegetables," wrote John Thorne, editor of *Simple Cooking,* "a simple soup is often a busy day's only enjoyable culinary challenge: to feed ourselves on something warm, filling, and nourishing, on a moment's notice and out of nothing much at all."

Soup is one of the earliest dishes of mankind; it was probably invented soon after the first utensils for boiling were invented. The root words for the word *soup* — *sop* and *sup* — originally meant the slice of bread onto which broth was poured. Before the advent of flour and bread, the only way soups could be thickened was with grains, which led to gruels and porridges.

We are not certain where spicy soups were invented, but a good bet is the Yucatán Peninsula, home of the Mayas. Since they combined chiles with numerous vegetables, it makes sense that soups were one of their options. After chile peppers were transferred to the Old World, it didn't take cooks long to discover that simply dropping a chile pod into a soup could spice it up and add a whole new dimension to eating.

Our hot and spicy and meatless soups begin with Hot Lemon Peel Soup with Roasted Garlic and Peppers, one of the most unusual soups we have encountered. It mixes the flavors and textures of garlic, citrus peel, tofu, bell peppers, and New Mexican red chile powder — a perfect soupy beginning.

Corn soups are next. That grain is mixed with the flavors of fennel, anise, tarragon, ginger, and jalapeños in our Opposites Attract Soup, so named by Melissa because of the unusual blending of those tastes. Grilled Corn Soup with Ancho Chile Cream, from chef Vincent Guerithault, combines French techniques with Southwestern flavors. Ancho is the perfect chile for this soup because of its raisiny flavor and mild heat. Green Chile Corn Chowder is a commonly served stew in New Mexico, where the cooks love to combine chiles with other New World crops such as corn and potatoes.

Ah, beans, the healthy musical fruit, follow in a trio of recipes. Black beans, Dave's favorite, are featured in a meatless marvel, Black Bean Bourbon Chili, where they are spiced by pasilla and chipotle chiles and further flavored with tomatoes and bourbon. Mary Jane offers her Beall Court Black Bean Soup, which she judges to be the best of the myriad of black bean soups prepared at her address. And Pungent Pinto Bean Soup with Red Chile Puree is a simple bean soup that is attractively decorated with the red chile puree.

Two mushroom soups follow. Sichuan Hot and Sour Mushroom Soup, from Richard Sterling, a contributing editor of *Chile Pepper* magazine, features two varieties of mushrooms, joined by piquin chiles and white pepper. Mushroom Cream Soup with a Chipotle Kick also has two varieties of mushrooms, but this time they are combined with chipotle chiles and Italian parsley.

We travel the world with our next four soups. Pasta e Fagioli, a Venetian bean-and-macaroni favorite, is considerably spiced up; Callaloo, from the Caribbean, includes habaneros, which figures. While in the tropics, why not experience A Taste of the Tropics Soup, with mangoes, coconut, and habaneros again? Then it's just a short hop over to Mexico for some Cheesy Chipotle Soup, where celery and carrots collide gracefully with chipotle chiles and cheddar cheese.

The next logical place to land is New Mexico, where our friends and neighbors never stop experimenting. Roll Over in Your Grave New Mexico Gumbo is a melding of the bayou and the arroyo, combining okra with New Mexican green chile and black-eyed peas. Tiffany's Bean Pot Soup, which hails from the late, lamented Tiffany's restaurant in Cerrillos, makes a spectacular comeback; the chameleon-like Chile-Cheese Bisque can be spiced up with any number of options. Ancho chiles and New Mexican chiles blend their flavors in Tortilla Soup Especiale — a fine example, from Melissa, of the myriad of tortilla soups.

After all that heat, let's cool off with our collection of cold soups. Heh, heh, even cold soups can be hot! Iced Nectarine Soup is infused with red chile powder; Sri Lankan Eggplant Surprise uses curry powder for its punch. Sandia Sunset Cucumber Soup combines paprika with chile powder; Spicy Gazpacho, from *Chile Pepper* European correspondent and contributing editor Sharon Hudgins, allows the cook to select a hot sauce to inflame the cool vegetables.

A full meal, not to mention an aroma-filled house, can be made by matching these soups with the spicy breads from Chapter 8 — but don't forget about the salads from Chapter 3!

HOT LEMON PEEL SOUP WITH ROASTED GARLIC AND PEPPERS

In our opinion, it's almost impossible to eat too much garlic. So if, like us, you're a lover of the "stinking rose," you'll enjoy this soup. It's guaranteed to keep away evil spirits and vampires — except in California, where the Gilroy Garlic Festival is held each year. There's so much garlic there that the aforementioned spirits and vamps may just drop in for a bite!

1 **whole head of garlic, separated into cloves**	8 **ounces soft tofu, drained and cut into 1-inch-long strips**
1 **tablespoon vegetable oil** **Pinch of basil**	1 **roasted red bell pepper, peeled, seeds and stems removed, cut into 1-inch-long strips**
6 **cups Rich Vegetable Stock (see recipe, p. 5)**	
1 **lemon peel (rind part only)**	3 **tablespoons New Mexico red chile powder**
1 **6-by-½-inch strip of orange peel**	**Minced basil for garnish**
1 **sprig basil**	

Preheat the oven to 375 degrees. Coat the garlic cloves with the oil in a small bowl. Place the garlic in a baking dish and bake until light brown, about 20 minutes. Remove the garlic from the oven and cool to room temperature. Then squeeze the garlic to release the cloves from their skins. Place the garlic in a food processor along with the remaining oil, the basil, and ¼ cup of the stock, and puree.

In a heavy medium saucepan, combine the rest of the vegetable stock, the lemon peel, the orange peel, and the sprig of basil. Bring the soup to a boil. Then add the garlic puree, tofu, red bell pepper, and red chile to the mixture. Reduce the heat and simmer, uncovered, for 5 minutes. Discard the peels and the sprig. Ladle into bowls and sprinkle with fresh basil.

Serves: 4
Heat Scale: Medium

OPPOSITES ATTRACT SOUP

Here's a creation from Melissa, who observes, "Ginger and tarragon may be two of the most different ingredients that I have ever put together in a soup. Add a little jalapeño and fennel and you've got a tastebud adventure in the making."

2	tablespoons olive oil	1	teaspoon lime juice
3	tablespoons minced ginger	¼	cup anise-flavored liqueur
2	jalapeño chiles, seeds and stems removed, minced	3	fennel bulbs, minced
		4½	cups Rich Vegetable Stock (see recipe, p. 5)
1	onion, finely chopped	1	fennel bulb, sliced
4	celery stalks, chopped	3	tablespoons minced fresh tarragon
1	teaspoon fennel seeds, ground		Salt to taste

In a large saucepan, heat the olive oil and add the ginger and jalapeños. Sauté briefly until the ingredients begin to soften. Add the onion, celery, fennel seeds, and lime juice and cook for about 3 minutes. Add the anise liqueur and simmer for 3 minutes. Add the minced fennel and the vegetable stock. Bring the soup to a boil and then cover. Turn down heat to simmer for 15 to 20 minutes, or until the vegetables are tender. In a food processor, puree the mixture in 3 parts. Return the puree to the pan and bring to a simmer, adding the sliced fennel. Simmer for 3 minutes. Serve in warm bowls and garnish with minced tarragon.

Serves: 6
Heat Scale: Medium

GRILLED CORN SOUP
WITH ANCHO CHILE CREAM

This recipe, by chef Vincent Guerithault, was featured in the "Hot Spots" department of *Chile Pepper* magazine. It shows his combination of French techniques with Southwestern ingredients. Dave and Mary Jane tasted it at the restaurant Vincent Guerithault on Camelback, in Phoenix.

THE SOUP

4	ears of corn, shucked	1	jalapeño chile, seeds and stem removed, minced
2	cloves garlic, minced		
½	cup finely chopped carrots	1½	cups Rich Vegetable Stock (see recipe, p. 5)
½	cup finely chopped onions	1	cup half-and-half
¼	cup finely chopped celery		

THE ANCHO CHILE CREAM

1	ancho chile, seeds and stems removed, shredded	3	tablespoons half-and-half
		1	tablespoon sour cream

Grill the ears of corn for 5 minutes over a hot flame. Remove, cool, and cut the kernels from the ears. Combine the corn, garlic, carrots, onions, celery, jalapeño, and stock; simmer for 30 minutes. Add the half-and-half, bring to a boil, and boil for 5 minutes.

To make the chile cream, simmer the ancho chile in the half-and-half for 5 minutes. Puree this mixture in a blender and let cool; then stir in the sour cream.

To serve, place the soup in bowls and swirl 1 tablespoon of blended ancho cream on top of the soup in each bowl.

Serves: 4
Heat Scale: Medium

GREEN CHILE CORN CHOWDER

Here's another corn treat that's rich, delicious — but not fat-free. However, you can do a 3-to-1 ratio of milk to cream and cut out a little of the fat. Since this is such a rich soup, we make it in the early fall, when the green chiles are fresh, and in the cold winter months, using the green chiles from the freezer. If you are using canned green chiles, rinse them thoroughly.

4 **cups corn kernels, fresh or frozen, cooked for a minute or two**

4 **tablespoons vegetable oil**

2½ **cups diced onion**

3 **cloves garlic, minced**

6 **large red potatoes, diced into ½-inch cubes (about 4 cups)**

4 **cups Rich Vegetable Stock (see recipe, p. 5)**

2 **cups chopped New Mexican green chiles**

2 **cups low fat milk**

2 **cups heavy cream**

Salt and pepper to taste

Puree 3 cups of the corn and set aside. In a large Dutch oven, sauté the onions in the oil for 2 to 3 minutes, then add the garlic and sauté for a minute more. Stir in the corn puree, the remaining 1 cup of corn kernels, the potatoes, and the stock; bring to a boil over a high heat. Reduce the heat to a simmer and partially cover the pot. Simmer 10 to 15 minutes, or until the potatoes are done.

Add the green chiles, the milk, and the cream — stirring constantly — and continue to stir until the mixture is heated through. Add salt and pepper to taste.

Serves: 10 to 12
Heat Scale: Medium

BLACK BEAN BOURBON CHILI

From Nancy Gerlach, food editor of *Chile Pepper* magazine, comes this interesting meatless black bean chili. She comments, "Beans are inexpensive and an excellent source of protein as well, making them one of the best nutritional bargains on the market. Add some flour tortillas and grated cheese, and they can't be beat."

3   **dried pasilla chiles, stems and seeds removed**

3   **dried chipotle chiles, stems removed**
   Hot water

1   **large onion, chopped**

1   **clove garlic, minced**

3   **tablespoons vegetable oil**

2   **cups black beans, soaked overnight**

3   **tomatoes, peeled and chopped**

3   **cups water**

¼   **cup bourbon (optional)**

1   **teaspoon ground cumin**
   Grated Monterey Jack cheese for a garnish (optional)

Cover the chiles with hot water and let them sit for 10 minutes to soften. Puree the chiles with the soaking water into a smooth paste.

Sauté the onion and garlic in the oil until soft. Add the pureed chiles, beans, tomatoes, and water. Bring to a boil, reduce the heat, stir in the bourbon (if desired), and simmer for 2½ to 3 hours or until done. Add the cumin and continue to cook for an additional 30 minutes.

Serve the chili in bowls, topped with the grated cheese.

Serves: 6
Heat Scale: Hot

BEALL COURT BLACK BEAN SOUP

Here's another black bean specialty. We know there are a million recipes for black bean soup, but, trust us, this one is special. It's an amalgam of Cuban style, Panama style, and Southwest style. To upgrade the heat, just add more chipotles in adobo sauce or ground pure New Mexican red chile. Serve it with hot buttered flour tortillas and Orange Gold Salad (see recipe, p. 71). Served in small bowls, it could be a first course, or, served in large bowls, it's a real meal! It can also be cooked down a little and served over rice as a filling, nutritious main course.

1 pound dried black beans	1 28-ounce can tomatoes, undrained
About 10 cups water	
1 whole bell pepper	2 tablespoons New Mexican chile powder
⅔ cup olive oil	
1 cup onion, diced	2 tablespoons chopped cilantro
4 cloves garlic, finely chopped	
	2 chipotle chiles in adobo sauce, minced
1 green bell pepper, diced	
½ teaspoon freshly ground black pepper	6 to 8 cups Rich Vegetable Stock (see recipe, p. 5)
1 tablespoon dried oregano	2 tablespoons white vinegar
1 bay leaf	
2 tablespoons sugar	2 tablespoons white wine
1 to 2 teaspoons ground cumin	2 tablespoons olive oil

Wash the beans and rinse thoroughly. Put them in a large, heavy pot with the water and the whole bell pepper and bring to a boil. Lower the heat to a simmer and cook for about 2½ hours, or until the beans are almost tender.

Heat the olive oil in a sauté pan and add the onion, garlic, and diced bell pepper; sauté for 2 minutes, or until the pepper is softened. Add to the cooked beans. Then add all the remaining ingredients except the last four, adding the vegetable stock as needed to keep a soupy consistency. Let the beans simmer slowly for about 45 minutes. Add the vinegar, wine, and olive oil and simmer the beans for another 45 minutes, adding more vegetable stock if necessary.

Serves: 6 to 8
Heat Scale: Medium

〰〰〰〰〰〰〰

PUNGENT PINTO BEAN SOUP
WITH RED CHILE PUREE

The beans in this soup contain protein and fiber, and the chile provides vitamins. This soup also looks as good as it tastes. The trick is swirling the red chile puree just right. Practice makes perfect!

2   **large, fresh New Mexican red chiles, roasted, peeled, and seeded (or substitute green chiles)**
1   **teaspoon vegetable oil**
2   **tablespoons olive oil**
2   **medium onions, chopped**
3   **cups cooked pinto beans, drained and rinsed**

2   **cups Rich Vegetable Stock (see recipe, p. 5)**
1   **cup half-and-half (or half-and-half substitute)**
½   **teaspoon salt**
½   **teaspoon freshly ground black pepper**

Place the chiles in a food processor with the vegetable oil and puree them. Set aside. In a large saucepan, heat the olive oil over medium-high heat. Add the onions and sauté until they are just golden. Turn the heat down to medium, add the beans, and continue to cook, stirring gently for another few minutes. Add the stock and cover the pan. Cook the soup for 15 minutes.

Puree the soup in batches in a food processor, then return the mixture to the saucepan. Over medium heat, add the half-and-half, salt, and pepper, and cook until completely heated through. Ladle the soup into warm soup bowls and place a tablespoon of the red chile puree on the top of each one. Swirl the puree into a spiral with a wooden spoon.

Serves: 6
Heat Scale: Mild

~~~~~~~~~~~~~~~

SICHUAN HOT AND SOUR MUSHROOM SOUP

Here's a delicious vegetarian version of a recipe from Richard Sterling, contributing editor of *Chile Pepper*. He notes, "The Chinese use white pepper extensively in noodle dishes and soups. This is an excellent soup for a cold winter's night in Sichuan or even a warm day in West Texas."

5 cups Rich Vegetable Stock (see recipe, p. 5)

6 wild mushrooms, such as chanterelles or morels, soaked in 1 cup water

¾ pound straw or white mushrooms or both, sliced

2 piquin chiles, left whole

1 tablespoon ground white pepper

2 tablespoons white vinegar

2 to 4 tablespoons soy sauce

1 dash dry sherry

1 tablespoon cornstarch combined with 2 tablespoons water

1 egg, beaten

¼ teaspoon sesame oil

2 scallions, minced

Combine the stock and the mushroom-soaking liquid in a pan and bring them to a boil. Add the mushrooms and piquin chiles. Cover and simmer 15 minutes. Add the pepper, vinegar, soy sauce, and sherry. Thicken with the cornstarch paste. Slowly add the beaten egg, stirring gently, and cook for 5 minutes. Sprinkle with the sesame oil and minced scallions. Remove the piquins before serving.

Serves: 6
Heat Scale: Mild

MUSHROOM CREAM SOUP
WITH A CHIPOTLE KICK

White button mushrooms form the base of another flavorful mushroom soup; the addition of the porcini mushrooms and the chipotle chile gives it zest and earthiness. Even though we simply take mushrooms for granted nowadays, in the early 1700s they were considered one of the decadent attractions of Paris!

2	tablespoons margarine
1	cup diced onion
¼	cup finely chopped celery
1	small clove garlic
½	teaspoon ground white pepper
1	pound finely chopped button mushrooms
2	tablespoons of rehydrated porcini or morel mushrooms (soaked, rinsed, and chopped)
¼	cup margarine
½	cup white flour
½	teaspoon salt

3	cups of Rich Vegetable Stock (see recipe, p. 5)
1¼	cups milk (or use ¾ cup milk and ½ cup half-and-half for a richer soup)
3	tablespoons chopped Italian parsley (or 2 tablespoons parsley and 1 tablespoon cilantro)
½	teaspoon dried thyme
½	teaspoon summer savory
2	chipotle chiles in adobo sauce, diced

Melt the 2 tablespoons of margarine in a large saucepan and sauté the onion, the celery, and the garlic; add the white pepper and the mushrooms and sauté until most of the mushroom liquid is gone. Remove from the heat.

In another saucepan, melt the ¼ cup of margarine, add the flour and salt, and cook the flour mixture for a minute or two, stirring constantly. Add the stock and whisk constantly until the mixture is thoroughly blended. Cook over a very low heat until the mixture has thickened slightly, whisking occasionally — about 3 to 4 minutes.

Add the stock-flour mixture to the sautéed mushroom mixture and heat at a simmer, while adding the remaining ingredients, for about 10 to 15 minutes or until heated through. Do not let the mixture boil. Season with additional salt to taste.

Serves: 4 to 6
Heat Scale: Medium

∿∿∿∿∿∿∿∿∿∿∿

PASTA E FAGIOLI

This pasta and bean soup is from Nanette Blanchard's article on hot and spicy Italian food that appeared in *Chile Pepper* magazine. Nanette noted, "Here is an unusual version of the traditional Venetian bean and macaroni soup. This version includes sun-dried tomatoes and zucchini with piquin chiles."

2 tablespoons olive oil
1 onion, chopped
3 cloves garlic, minced
2 zucchinis, sliced thinly
2 tablespoons crushed hot red chiles, such as piquins
6 sun-dried tomatoes marinated in oil, drained, and chopped
4 cups cooked and drained cannellini beans

3 cups cooked macaroni
4 cups Rich Vegetable Stock (see recipe, p. 5)
2 teaspoons dried oregano
Salt and freshly ground black pepper to taste
Grated Parmesan and extra-virgin olive oil for garnish

Heat the oil in a saucepan and sauté the onion for several minutes or until soft. Add the garlic and zucchinis and continue cooking, stirring occasionally, until zucchinis are tender. Add the chile and tomatoes; sauté for an additional 3 minutes.

Stir in the beans, macaroni, stock, and oregano. Season to taste. Cover and simmer over medium heat for 15 minutes. Garnish each bowl with grated Parmesan and a drizzle of good extra-virgin olive oil, if desired.

Serves: 10
Heat Scale: Medium

∿∿∿∿∿∿∿∿∿∿∿

CALLALOO

This remarkable bright-green soup is often called the "national dish" of Trinidad and Tobago. Dave and Mary Jane tried it often on their trip to that country and collected this recipe from chefs Keith Toby and Irvine Jackson of the Cafe Savannah. It features callaloo (taro leaves or dasheen), but spinach is an excellent substitute.

3   bundles callaloo or 3 bunches fresh spinach, washed, tough ribs removed, coarsely chopped
4   cups canned unsweetened coconut milk (available in Asian markets and gourmet shops)
2   cups milk
2   cloves garlic, minced

2   medium onions, chopped
1   bunch scallions, chopped
¼   pound Hubbard or acorn squash, peeled and coarsely chopped
¼   pound margarine
½   habanero chile, seeds and stem removed, minced
    Salt and pepper to taste

In a stockpot or soup pot, combine all the ingredients and boil for 4 minutes. Reduce the heat and simmer for 40 minutes. If too thick, add more coconut milk. Remove from the heat, cool, and puree in a blender in small batches. Reheat the soup and serve.

Serves: 8 to 10
Heat Scale: Medium

A TASTE OF THE TROPICS SOUP

This rich and colorful mango-coconut soup will deliver you directly to the islands! It is interesting in that it is a fruit soup spiced with a chile that has a fruity aroma, the habanero.

1	ripe mango, peeled, seeded, and halved	½	fresh habanero chile, seeds and stem removed, minced
1	vanilla bean	⅔	cup half-and-half
½	cup cream of coconut (available in the mixed-drink section of the grocery store)	2	to 4 tablespoons sugar Shredded coconut and sprigs of mint for garnish
1½	cups water		

Cut the mango into large chunks and puree in a food processor until almost smooth. A few small pieces should remain. Cut the vanilla bean in half and scrape the seeds into a medium-sized saucepan. Add the mango puree, cream of coconut, water, chile, half-and-half, and sugar. Cook over medium heat, uncovered, for 5 minutes. Lower the heat and continue to simmer, uncovered, stirring occasionally, for 5 minutes. Remove the vanilla beans and serve the soup in warm bowls. Garnish with shredded coconut and mint springs.

Serves: 4
Heat Scale: Medium

〰〰〰〰〰〰〰

CHEESY CHIPOTLE SOUP

This soup, imported from Mexico and changed a little, is smooth and goes down easily, with just a little afterburn. We like it because it actually tastes better as a leftover!

1	stick margarine	½	cup flour
2	chipotle chiles in adobo sauce, chopped	3	cups Rich Vegetable Stock (see recipe, p. 5)
2	carrots, peeled and shredded	½	teaspoon ground white pepper
2	stalks celery, finely chopped	2½	cups milk
1	small onion, finely chopped	2	cups grated cheddar cheese
1	cup finely chopped broccoli	2	teaspoons brown sugar
1	clove garlic, minced	¼	cup slivered almonds

Melt the margarine in a medium saucepan. Place the chipotles, carrots, celery, onion, broccoli, and garlic in the pan and sauté over medium heat for about 6 minutes, stirring constantly. Sprinkle the flour over the sautéed mixture and mix in. Slowly add the stock and ground pepper and simmer, uncovered, over low heat for 20 minutes. Add the milk, cheese, and brown sugar. Cook over low heat for 10 minutes. Garnish with the almonds.

Serves: 6
Heat Scale: Medium

〜〜〜〜〜〜〜〜〜〜

ROLL OVER IN YOUR GRAVE NEW MEXICO GUMBO

This recipe is so named because that's exactly what our friends in New Orleans will do when they hear about this one! They think gumbo is synonymous with seafood! However, this gumbo is rich with the flavor of okra and chiles, and that's what gives it punch. Also, searing the mushrooms with the onions gives a certain richness to the dish. Serve it with garlic-infused French bread and a big green salad or a spicy fruit salad.

2	tablespoons olive oil	1	cup chopped New Mexican green chiles
2	medium onions, chopped		
½	pound mushrooms, cleaned and sliced	1	bay leaf
3	cloves garlic, minced	2	cups cooked black-eyed peas (or substitute 1 16-ounce can, drained and rinsed)
1	pound fresh tomatoes, peeled, seeded, and diced (or substitute 1 16-ounce can of tomatoes, diced, with juice)		
		3	tablespoons minced fresh parsley
2	cups tomato juice or V-8 juice	2	tablespoons New Mexican red chile powder
1	pound fresh okra, cleaned and chopped (or substitute 1 15-ounce package frozen okra, thawed and chopped)	1	to 2 cups Rich Vegetable Stock (see recipe, p. 5)
		4	cups cooked rice

In a large, heavy Dutch oven, heat the olive oil. When the oil is hot, add the onions and sauté for a minute. Then add the sliced mushrooms and sauté until they give off their juices and start to brown. Add the garlic and stir it in. Then add the chopped tomatoes with their juices and sauté for 10 minutes.

Add the tomato juice, okra, green chiles, and bay leaf. Cover and simmer for 30 minutes; check for burning and stir once or twice. Add some stock if necessary.

Add the black-eyed peas, the parsley, the red chile, and 1 cup of the stock. Simmer for 30 minutes, covered, stirring occasionally. Check the consistency; it should be thick and soup-like. Add more stock if necessary.

Place a portion of the hot rice in a large soup bowl and pour some of the gumbo over the top. Serve hot and spicy!

Serves: 8 to 10
Heat Scale: Medium

∿∿∿∿∿∿∿∿∿

TIFFANY'S BEAN POT SOUP

Ahh, it's the weekend! We'll drive to Cerrillos, New Mexico, dine at Tiffany's Restaurant, and watch a hokey melodrama along with the tourists and many of the locals. But since the whole complex burned down many years ago, all we have now are great dining memories and Tiffany's recipe for bean soup. It's a great escape into the past of 20 years ago. This soup freezes well, so make the whole recipe; it doesn't seem to have the same flavor when the recipe is quartered or halved.

2   cups dried pinto beans, cleaned
½   cup soy bacon bits
1   quart water
1   22-ounce can tomato juice
4   cups Rich Vegetable Stock (see recipe, p. 5)
3   onions, chopped
3   cloves garlic, minced
3   tablespoons chopped parsley
¼   cup chopped green bell pepper

2   serrano or jalapeño chiles, seeds and stems removed, chopped
4   tablespoons brown sugar
1   tablespoon New Mexican red chile powder
1   teaspoon salt
1   teaspoon crushed bay leaves
1   teaspoon oregano
½   teaspoon ground cumin
½   teaspoon crushed rosemary
½   teaspoon celery seed

½	teaspoon ground thyme	4	whole cloves
½	teaspoon ground marjoram	1	cup dry sherry
½	teaspoon basil	1	cup chopped green onions for garnish
½	teaspoon curry powder		

Soak the beans overnight and then drain. Add all the other ingredients except the sherry.

Bring the mixture to a boil, then lower the heat to simmer and cook slowly for 2 to 3 hours, until the beans are tender. Add the sherry just before serving.

Serve in large soup bowls, topped with the chopped green onions.

Serves: 8 to 10
Heat Scale: Medium

Red Hots

There is a superstition that chile peppers grow better if they are planted by a red-headed or high-tempered person. The *Journal of American Folklore* illustrated the fable with a tale told by a former slave in the Deep South: "My old woman and me had a spat and I went right out and planted my peppers and they came right up."

CHILE-CHEESE BISQUE

There are many different kinds of chile that can be added to this bisque. Add New Mexico green chile for a color contrast and a zip to the tongue; use chipotle chiles in adobo sauce for a spicy, smoky flavor; or add 2 tablespoons pure red chile powder for yet another taste treat. The spicy flavor of this bisque can be varied according to what the rest of the menu will be — and all of the chile, of course, goes well with Pumpkin Bread (see recipe, p. 203).

3	tablespoons margarine
½	cup diced onion
¼	cup diced celery
½	cup chopped carrot
2	tablespoons flour
½	teaspoon cornstarch
4	cups Rich Vegetable Stock (see recipe, p. 5)
4	cups low-fat milk
¹⁄₁₆	teaspoon baking soda
1	pound sharp cheddar cheese, cubed
½	cup diced New Mexico green chiles (or 1 or 2 chipotle chiles in adobo sauce, or 2 tablespoons New Mexican red chile powder)
	Salt and freshly ground black pepper to taste
1½	cups boiled potatoes, diced into ½-inch cubes
3	tablespoons cilantro, minced for garnish

Sauté the onion, celery, and carrots in the melted margarine until tender.

Add the flour and cornstarch and cook until the mixture bubbles. Add the stock and milk to make a smooth sauce. Add the soda; gradually add the cubed cheese and chile. Taste the soup and season to taste with the salt and the freshly ground black pepper. Over a very low heat, stir until the cheese is melted. Just before serving, add the diced potatoes and cook until they are heated through. Ladle the soup into heated bowls and sprinkle the garnish of cilantro on top.

Serves: 6 to 8
Heat Scale: Medium

TORTILLA SOUP ESPECIALE

Here is one of Melissa's all-time favorite soups. She writes, "In most restaurants it is served as a first course, but I like it so much we usually make it a meal all by itself! Favor your guests with warm flour tortillas with red chile honey, and you'll have quite a meal!"

6 ancho chiles, seeds and stems removed

3 New Mexican green chiles, roasted, peeled, seeds and stems removed

1 pound tomatoes, diced

1 medium onion, chopped into large chunks

6 large garlic cloves

½ cup safflower oil

1 teaspoon fresh oregano (or ½ teaspoon dried oregano)

8 cups Rich Vegetable Stock (see recipe, p. 5)

1 tablespoon lime juice
  Safflower oil (for deep frying)

7 6-inch corn tortillas, cut into 6 strips each
  Monterey Jack cheese, grated, for garnish
  Low-fat sour cream, for garnish

1 lime, cut into thin round slices, for garnish
  Avocados, peeled, pitted, and diced, for garnish (optional)

Place the ancho and New Mexican chiles in a food processor and chop to a fine consistency. Remove to a bowl. Place tomatoes, onions, and garlic in the processor and chop coarsely, using the on/off switch.

Heat the oil in a deep skillet over medium-high heat. Add the chopped chiles, the tomato mixture, and the oregano. Cook for 10 minutes, uncovered, over medium heat, stirring continually. Remove from the heat and puree the mixture in the blender in 4 batches, adding vegetable stock as necessary if the mixture is very thick. Strain the puree into a heavy, large saucepan. Add the remaining stock and lime juice and cook, uncovered, stirring occasionally, over medium heat until it is reduced slightly, about 15 to 20 minutes.

In a deep frying pan, heat the vegetable oil to 375 degrees. Add one third of the tortilla strips and fry until golden brown. Using a slotted spoon, transfer the strips to paper towels to drain. Repeat until all of the tortilla strips are fried.

Spoon the soup into bowls and add tortilla strips. Then top with a sprinkling of cheese, a dollop of sour cream, a lime slice, and a spoonful of avocado (optional).

Serves: 8
Heat Scale: Medium

∿∿∿∿∿∿∿∿

ICED NECTARINE SOUP

This is one of most unusual soups we've ever encountered — fruity, cold, and spicy all at the same time. Feel free to experiment with different chile powders for different flavors.

8   medium nectarines, peeled and pitted
12 ounces peach yogurt
½   cup Riesling wine
2   tablespoons port wine

2   tablespoons New Mexican red chile powder
¼   teaspoon ground ginger
    Mint leaves for garnish

Cut seven of the nectarines into small cubes. Quarter the remaining one and put it aside in the refrigerator to be used later as a garnish.

Puree the cubed nectarines in a food processor. Add the remaining ingredients, except the mint, and whisk until thoroughly blended. Refrigerate for 4 to 6 hours. Serve in cold bowls, garnished with the nectarine quarters and mint leaves.

Serves: 4
Heat Scale: Mild

SRI LANKAN EGGPLANT SURPRISE

This soup — fresh with hints of old Ceylon — marries the exotic textures and tastes of curry, eggplant, and lime. To increase the heat, add more piquins, but be sure to remove them before serving.

4 tablespoons margarine	½ cup plain low-fat yogurt
1 medium onion, chopped	½ teaspoon salt
1 tablespoon curry powder	¼ teaspoon lemon pepper
1 eggplant, peeled and cut into ½-inch cubes	Thinly sliced lime sections and chopped
4 cups vegetable broth	parsley for garnish
2 small hot chiles, such as piquins, left whole	

Melt the margarine in a saucepan over medium heat. Add the onions and sauté until soft, about 4 minutes. Stir in the curry powder and reduce the heat to low. Stir for a few minutes, then add the eggplant, broth, and chiles. Heat the mixture until it boils, then reduce the heat and simmer, covered, until the eggplant is soft, about 45 minutes. Remove the chiles and discard.

Remove the eggplant from the heat, allow it to cool somewhat, then puree the soup in a food processor while still warm. Stir the yogurt, salt, and lemon pepper into the puree. Cool the soup to room temperature and refrigerate it, covered, for at least 4 hours. To serve, ladle it into bowls and garnish with the lime and parsley.

Serves: 4
Heat Scale: Medium

SANDIA SUNSET CUCUMBER SOUP

A great cold and spicy treat! We've nicknamed it *sandia,* the Spanish word for watermelon because the soup takes on a pink hue from the paprika and the red chile. Also, here in Albuquerque, at sunset, everyone watches the Sandia Mountains change from black to pink as the setting sun hits them for a perfect two or three minutes of "watermelon" color. We prefer Italian parsley to the "grocery" variety, because it has more zest and flavor. It is easy to grow, even in a pot at a sunny window — unless you have cats who like to graze, like ours! (So we just grow it year-round in the greenhouse.)

4	cups Rich Vegetable Stock (see recipe, p. 5)	1	teaspoon paprika (we prefer Szeged Hungarian; it's not bitter)
1½	cups cucumbers, peeled, seeded, and diced	1	tablespoon dried dill
½	cup finely diced onion	2	serrano chiles, seeds and stems removed, finely chopped
1	clove garlic, minced		
½	teaspoon ground white pepper	1	cup plain yogurt
¼	teaspoon salt	3	tablespoons chopped Italian parsley for garnish
2	whole cloves		
1	teaspoon New Mexican red chile powder		

In a large saucepan, bring the vegetable stock to a full boil and add the cucumbers, onion, garlic, pepper, salt, cloves, red chile powder, and paprika. Reduce the heat and simmer, uncovered, for 10 minutes. Remove the whole cloves.

Add the remaining ingredients and, using a potato masher, mash everything until it is very coarse in texture.

At this point, the soup can be chilled and served. Or it can be heated slowly and served warm. Just don't let it boil, because the yogurt will curdle.

Serves: 4 to 6
Heat Scale: Medium

▼▲▼▲▼▲▼▲▼▲▼▲▼▲▼▲▼▲▼▲▼

Food Habits, The Sequel

Sales of gourmet foods topped $22 billion in 1989 and are expected to reach $39 billion by 1995 — which translates into a staggering $500 per U.S. household spent on specialty food items. Also, there has been a vast increase in the number of produce products appearing in supermarkets. A decade ago, an average of about 70 products were stocked; today, the average number stocked is 250, which may rise to 450 by the end of this decade.

▼▲▼▲▼▲▼▲▼▲▼▲▼▲▼▲▼▲▼▲▼

SPICY GAZPACHO
(ANDALUSIAN COLD TOMATO SOUP)

From Sharon Hudgins, who collected this recipe while on assignment in Spain for *Chile Pepper* magazine, comes this observation: *"Gazpacho was originally a simple peasant dish, consisting only of bread, garlic, salt, vinegar, oil, and water. After the discovery of the New World, tomatoes and peppers were also included. The following is a recipe for classic tomato-based gazpacho, the best-known version of this soup. But the Spaniards have dozens of soups called gazpacho — cold or hot; thick or thin; red, white, green, or yellow; made from a wide range of ingredients."* Serve the chilled *gazpacho* in individual soup bowls and pass around small bowls of various garnishes to sprinkle on top of the *gazpacho,* according to the diner's choice.

1 green bell pepper, seeded and deveined, coarsely chopped

1 red bell pepper, seeded and deveined, coarsely chopped

6 medium-sized ripe tomatoes, preferably fresh (if not, use canned ones and use their juice in place of the tomato juice, below)

1 large onion

2 medium cucumbers, peeled

3 cloves garlic

1 cup coarsely crumbled, crustless French bread

2 tablespoons tomato paste

3 cups tomato juice

6 tablespoons olive oil

1/4 cup red wine vinegar

1 tablespoon mild Spanish paprika

1 to 2 teaspoons salt

1/8 teaspoon cumin

Bottled hot sauce to taste

Garnishes: 1/2 cup chopped onion, or spring onions sliced into thin rings; 1/2 cup each chopped green, red, and yellow bell peppers; 1/2 cup peeled and chopped cucumber; 1/4 cup chopped chives; 1 to 2 cups fried croutons

Puree the bell peppers, tomatoes, onion, cucumbers, garlic, and bread together in a food processor or blender. (Process the ingredients in batches, if necessary.) Transfer the pureed ingredients to a large bowl. Dissolve the tomato paste in the tomato juice and add to the pureed ingredients; mix well. Whisk in the olive oil, wine vinegar, paprika, salt, and cumin, until all ingredients are thoroughly combined. Cover and refrigerate for several hours before serving. Serve cold. Add hot sauce to taste, and use several garnishes (we recommend using at least four).

Serves: 8 to 10
Heat Scale: Varies

Lively Legumes and the Grains of Paradise

I n this chapter we reveal how well beans, other legumes, and grains such as rice fit into our hot and spicy and meatless plan. Such meals were long dismissed as "peasant food," but during the past decade or so they have been given their due. As registered dietitian Nancy Gerlach points out, "Legumes are a delicious, inexpensive source of high quality nutrition. They are low in calories, sodium, and fat while being a good source of complex carbohydrates, iron, potassium, calcium, B vitamins, and dietary fiber."

Beans also contain about 25 percent protein, but that protein lacks some essential amino acids and thus is regarded as "incomplete" protein. Interestingly enough, many nutritionists recommend serving beans with grains because the two foods together provide complete protein. Hence, our combination recipes, such as Mobay Rice and Peas, and Gallo Pinto, provide excellent protein and are some of the best meat substitutes around.

Speaking of rice, Americans are accustomed to eating one or two kinds, but in reality there are hundreds of varieties around the world. As exotic food expert Elizabeth Schneider points out, "They run from creamy to chewy, pearly white to deep umber, from delicately sweet to richly nutty; and they can be far more flavorful and texturally interesting than white rice." The best place to search for exotic rices is in Asian markets, and cooks should experiment with them. One of our favorite rices is *basmati,* usually imported from India or Pakistan. However, it is now being grown in Texas and is marketed as Texmati rice.

Our recipes in this chapter begin with beans and peas. Frijoles a la Charra, or ranch beans, is a recipe collected by our friend Robb Walsh at Don Limon's restaurant in Austin. East Coast Native Americans are given credit for inventing succotash, but we have given it a regional twist in our Southwestern Succotash. Adzuki beans, originally from Japan, are the star of Bean and Summer Squash Bake, and Chinese medicine says they are better for the kidneys than kidney beans!

Two of our bean recipes contain rice — Mobay Rice and Peas from Jamaica, and Gallo Pinto from Costa Rica. Both recipes were collected on location by Dave and Mary Jane. Lemony Hot String Beans with Chipotles is a splendid combination of flavors that features smoke-dried jalapeños combined with fresh beans. Bean dumplings take center stage in Mangia Fagioli Red-Hot Gnocchi, and chickpeas take over in Southwestern Spiced Garbanzos.

Lentil lovers will rejoice at our lentil matching of a soup and main dish. Curried Lentil Soup, which can be served over rice for that legume-rice protein combo, is charged up with curry powder and serranos. Lively Lentil Bake also combines lentils and rice — flavored and spiced with New Mexican chile.

Our rice dishes are a world tour of that grain, beginning with Mexicali Rice, our version of a Mexican favorite. Kabul Party Rice, from Afghanistan, was collected on location by our friend Arnold Krochmal. Pilaf-lover Dave reveals his secret rice recipe, Pilaf on the Pecos ("Green chile and piñons are the key," says he). Hot Green Risotto, another combination of the tastes of Italy and the Southwest, features imported *arborio* rice; Yellow Festive Rice, from Singapore, is flavored with curry spices and coconut milk.

A granary miscellany fills out this chapter. Tangy Tabuli, with bulgur wheat and fresh hot chiles, never fails to please guests; Bodacious Barley Bake combines the barley with carrots, bell peppers, piñons, and red chile powder. Couscous, that tiny semolina grain, is the star of Veggie Couscous with Mediterranean Harissa, which hails from North Africa via our garden. Curried Kasha with Vegetables is made with buckwheat groats — technically not a grain, but who cares? And Daring Dhal, a hybrid of Bombay and El Paso, combines lentils and pinto beans for an unusual collision of cultures.

FRIJOLES A LA CHARRA

This recipe, from Don Limon's Restaurant in Austin, Texas, was collected by our friend Robb Walsh, who is food editor of the *Austin Chronicle*. Robb says that Tex-Mex is back — and better than ever — and we believe him. We have substituted vegetable oil for animal fat in our version of the Don's recipe.

¼ cup olive oil

3 jalapeño chiles, stems and seeds removed, chopped fine (add more if you like things quite spicy)

1 small onion, diced

1 quart cooked pinto beans, along with the juice

1 large tomato, chopped

¼ teaspoon garlic powder Freshly ground black pepper to taste

2 tablespoons chopped fresh cilantro

Heat the oil and sauté the jalapeños and onion until well browned. Add the beans in their juice, tomato, garlic, and black pepper. Bring to a boil, add the cilantro, reduce the heat, and simmer, uncovered, for 15 minutes.

Serves: 6
Heat Scale: Medium to Hot

~~~~~~~~~~~~~~~

SOUTHWESTERN SUCCOTASH

Here is one answer to a bountiful garden harvest — combine those beans with corn and chile. This is a truly New World vegetable combination — and colorful, too!

3	tablespoons margarine	1	cup cooked corn kernels
¼	cup minced red bell pepper	¼	cup chopped New Mexican green chiles
1	cup cooked lima beans	1	teaspoon minced cilantro

Melt the margarine in a saucepan, add the red bell pepper, and sauté for 1 minute. Add the lima beans, corn, and green chiles. Sauté, stirring occasionally, for 5 minutes.

Stir in the cilantro right before serving.

Serves: 4
Heat Scale: Medium

〜〜〜〜〜〜〜〜〜〜〜〜

BEAN AND SUMMER SQUASH BAKE

This low-calorie entree will fill you up — but not out — during swimsuit season! Serve it with one of the salads from Chapter 3 and a bread from Chapter 8.

1	cup dry adzuki beans	2½	cups yellow squash, peeled and cubed
2½	cups water	½	cup chopped New Mexican green chiles
½	bay leaf	2	tablespoons barley miso, thinned with 2 tablespoons of water
1	teaspoon tarragon		
1	teaspoon olive oil		
1	onion, diced		
1	clove garlic, minced		

In a bowl, soak the beans for 2 to 3 hours. Discard the soaking water. In a large pot, place 2½ cups fresh water, the bay leaf, the tarragon, and the beans. Simmer, covered, for 2½ hours. During the last ½ hour that the beans are cooking, heat the oil in a medium pan and sauté the onion and garlic until tender. Add the yellow squash, chiles, and sea salt.

Sauté briefly, then reduce the heat and cook the squash until it is slightly tender, but not mushy. Once the squash is cooked, set it aside.

Preheat the oven to 375 degrees. Drain the beans and place them in a large casserole dish along with the miso thinned with water. Stir in the squash mixture, cover, and bake for 30 to 40 minutes.

Serves: 4 to 5
Heat Scale: Medium

〜〜〜〜〜〜〜〜〜

MOBAY RICE AND PEAS

Dave and Mary Jane collected this recipe on a trip to Ocho Rios. The peas in the dish are actually red kidney beans, and the dish is a staple in many Caribbean countries, including Jamaica, Cuba, and Haiti. The chile pepper normally used is the Scotch bonnet, but serranos, jalapeños, or hot New Mexican green chiles can be substituted. This dish has become a traditional Sunday brunch/lunch favorite in Jamaica.

1½	cups grated coconut meat	1	scallion, minced
4	cups water	1	3-inch sprig fresh thyme
1	cup dried red kidney beans, rinsed and cleaned	2	tablespoons minced habanero chile
1	clove garlic, crushed	2	cups long-grain rice
		2	cups water

Add the coconut meat to the 4 cups of water; stir and strain through cheesecloth or a fine sieve into a heavy Dutch oven. Add the beans and bring to a boil, then simmer, covered, for about 2 hours. Add the fresh seasonings and simmer for 2 minutes. Add the rice and 2 cups of water and bring to a boil. (There should be some coconut liquid left with the beans. If there isn't, add 1 or 2 extra cups of water to finish cooking the rice.) Then cover, reduce the heat, and cook until the liquid is absorbed, about 25 to 30 minutes. Remove from the heat for 10 minutes before serving.

Serves: 6
Heat Scale: Medium

~~~~~~~~~~~~~~~~~

GALLO PINTO

Gallo pinto, a Central American version of beans and rice, could be called the "national dish" of Costa Rica; it is served at breakfast, lunch, and dinner. As with any dish this popular, everyone has a personal version. David Tucker of the Hotel La Mariposa was kind enough to share his recipe with us during a vacation trip to Quepos, on the western coast.

1	cup black beans	½	cup chopped onion
1	bay leaf	⅓	cup chopped red bell pepper
4	tablespoons vegetable oil	1	tablespoon soy sauce
¼	teaspoon ground cumin, or to taste	1	teaspoon brown sugar
¼	teaspoon dried oregano, or to taste	1	teaspoon Lea & Perrins steak sauce
1	clove garlic	½	teaspoon Tabasco or other Louisiana hot sauce (or more, to taste)
½	teaspoon curry powder Pepper and salt to taste	1½	cups cooked rice

Cover the beans with water and soak for at least 4 hours. Rinse and add fresh cold water to cover. Bring the water to a boil. Add the bay leaf, 3 tablespoons of the oil, the cumin, the oregano, the garlic, and the curry powder. Reduce the heat and simmer for an hour or until the beans are soft. Season with the pepper and salt. Drain the beans and reserve the liquid.

Sauté the onion and pepper in the remaining oil until soft. Add the remaining ingredients.

Combine the beans with the cooked rice mixture. If the mixture is too stiff, add a little of the bean water or Rich Vegetable Stock (see recipe, p. 5) to achieve the desired consistency.

Serves: 4
Heat Scale: Mild

~~~~~~~~~~~~~~~

LEMONY HOT STRING BEANS WITH CHIPOTLES

This recipe is from Melissa, who brags, "I love this dish simply because it is made with string beans, the first vegetable I ever grew successfully in a garden — at the tender age of six. I didn't eat them with chipotles then, but they're awfully good that way now."

1 **pound string beans, trimmed and cut in half**	2 **chipotle chiles in adobo sauce, chopped**
2 **tablespoons safflower oil**	**Juice of 2 lemons**
2 **cloves garlic, minced**	**Parsley for garnish**

Steam the beans until tender, but still crisp. In a large skillet, heat the oil and quickly sauté the garlic. Add the chipotles to the mixture and stir. Next, add the string beans and sauté for 45 seconds. Remove the pan from the heat and squeeze the juice from the lemons onto the beans. Sprinkle with parsley and serve.

Serves: 6
Heat Scale: Medium

MANGIA FAGIOLI RED-HOT GNOCCHI

Roughly translated, the name of this Italian dish means "The bean-eater's red-hot gnocchi." These oval dumplings work well as a side dish or as a main event. We like them served simply, sprinkled with Parmesan cheese and a dash of Tabasco, but if you're feeling a bit Italian, toss them in any of the pasta sauces in Chapter 1.

2 **cups cooked navy beans, drained, pureed, and sieved**	¼ **teaspoon nutmeg**
	¼ **cup flour**
1 **teaspoon minced garlic**	1 **stick margarine**
1 **jalapeño chile, seeds and stem removed, minced**	½ **cup grated Parmesan cheese**

Preheat the oven to 375 degrees. Place the bean puree in a saucepan over medium heat, stirring continually. Mix the garlic, jalapeño, nutmeg, and flour into the mixture. Continue to beat until the mixture is very smooth and fluffy.

Grease a medium-sized baking dish. Melt the stick of margarine and place it in a small bowl. Using two tablespoons dipped in the melted margarine, scoop up a portion of the mixture and shape it into oval dumplings. Place the dumplings side by side in the baking dish. Continue the process until all of the mixture is used. Sprinkle the gnocchi with the remaining margarine and Parmesan. Bake, covered, for 20 to 30 minutes or until golden brown.

Serves: 6
Heat Scale: Mild

SOUTHWESTERN SPICED GARBANZOS

The early Spanish explorers and settlers introduced the garbanzo bean (also called the chickpea) into the Southwest centuries ago. By adding a little red chile, you can conjure up a simple but powerful side dish.

2 tablespoons vegetable oil	½ teaspoon basil
2 onions, chopped	2 teaspoons New Mexican red chile powder
4 cloves garlic, minced	½ teaspoon oregano
3 cups cooked garbanzo beans	1 tablespoon cilantro, minced
1 14-ounce can stewed tomatoes, chopped (reserve the liquid)	½ teaspoon dried cumin

Heat the oil in a large, deep pan. Sauté the onions in the pan over low heat until they are very tender. Add the garlic, stirring the mixture until the onions turn golden. Add the garbanzos, tomatoes (and their liquid), basil, red chile, oregano, cilantro, and dried cumin. Cover and simmer over low heat for 25 minutes until thick. Serve as is, or over freshly cooked rice.

Serves: 4 to 6
Heat Scale: Mild

CURRIED LENTIL SOUP

This soup could be the first course in an Indian-style dinner or, served over cooked rice in large bowls, it would constitute a hearty meal in itself, along with Spicy Cold Cucumber Salad (see recipe, p. 81). It tastes great all year 'round — it is also surprisingly refreshing in the hot summer months. It should actually be in the soup chapter, but we moved it over here to start out our duo of hot and spicy lentil dishes.

1 tablespoon olive oil
1 large onion, chopped
2 cloves garlic, chopped
5 scallions, sliced
½ cup diced celery
½ cup sliced carrots
1 jalapeño or serrano chile, seeds and stem removed, chopped
5 cups water
1 cup lentils, washed and sorted
1 teaspoon ground coriander
1 teaspoon turmeric
½ teaspoon ground cumin
½ teaspoon cayenne powder
1 teaspoon paprika
¼ teaspoon ground ginger (or 1 teaspoon freshly grated ginger)
1 tablespoon tamari soy sauce
¼ cup chopped cilantro, for garnish

Heat the olive oil in a medium-sized Dutch oven. Add the onions, garlic, and scallions and sauté for a minute. Then add the celery, carrots, and jalapeño (or serrano) and sauté for another minute.

Add the water, lentils, and all of the remaining ingredients (except the cilantro) and bring to a boil. Stir the mixture and lower the heat, cover, and simmer for an hour or until the lentils are soft but not mushy.

Remove from the heat, spoon into bowls, and garnish with the cilantro.

Serves: 6
Heat Scale: Mild

LIVELY LENTIL BAKE

This herbed lentil-and-rice casserole is the "main course" in our lentil duo. It's nutritious, versatile, and easy to make. It can be served as a casserole with a green, leafy salad and garlic bread, or it can be used to stuff bell peppers. If you have a garden, plant some Mexi-Bell green peppers; they have just a little bit of heat, and make a tasty change from the ordinary green bells.

4 ounces grated Swiss or Monterey Jack cheese

3 cups Rich Vegetable Stock (see recipe, p. 5)

¾ cup dry lentils, cleaned and washed

¾ cup chopped onion

½ cup long-grain brown rice

¼ cup dry white wine

½ cup chopped New Mexican green chiles

½ teaspoon basil

¼ teaspoon salt (optional)

½ teaspoon oregano

½ teaspoon thyme

1 clove garlic, minced

⅛ teaspoon freshly ground black pepper

Divide the cheese into 2 portions.

Combine all of the ingredients and half of the cheese and mix. Turn the mixture into an ungreased 1½-quart casserole. Bake in a 350-degree oven for 1½ hours, stirring twice while mixture is baking.

When the lentil-rice mixture is done, place the reserved cheese on top of the casserole and place back in the oven until the cheese melts.

Serves: 4 to 5
Heat Scale: Medium

MEXICALI RICE

Unlike other versions of Spanish rice, which tend to be bland tomato sauce concoctions, ours is crispy and lively with taste. Serve it with Very Verde Enchiladas (see recipe, p. 152) or with spicy grilled vegetables.

3 tablespoons Chile-Infused Oil (see recipe, p. 6)	2 jalapeño or serrano chiles, seeds and stems removed, chopped
1 cup uncooked rice	2 tablespoons chopped fresh cilantro
1 onion, chopped	
½ cup celery, diced	1 teaspoon fresh lime juice
¼ cup diced bell pepper	½ teaspoon oregano
1 clove garlic, minced	2 cups Rich Vegetable Stock (see recipe, p. 5)
2 large tomatoes, peeled, seeded, and coarsely chopped	1 cup grated sharp cheddar cheese (optional)

Heat the oil in a skillet and sauté the rice over low heat for 4 to 5 minutes, until it is golden. Add the onion, celery, bell pepper, and garlic and sauté for 1 minute. Add the remaining ingredients (except the cheese), stir, then bring the mixture to a boil. Cover with a tight-fitting lid, turn the heat down to a simmer, and cook for 20 minutes.

Optional: When the rice is done, spread the grated cheese over the top and cover until the cheese melts.

Serves: 4 to 6
Heat Scale: Medium

KABUL PARTY RICE

This party rice comes from our friend Arnold Krochmal, who was assigned to an agricultural experiment station in Afganistan in the 1950s. He commented on this recipe in *Chile Pepper* magazine: "This is a special dish prepared for celebrations when guests are expected. If pine nuts aren't available, pistachios can be substituted."

2	large carrots, peeled and grated
4	tablespoons margarine
3	large onions, chopped
2½	cups cooked white rice
½	cup shelled piñons or pine nuts
1	tablespoon chopped serrano or jalapeño chiles
½	cup seedless raisins
1	teaspoon each: ground cinnamon, cloves, cardamom, cumin

Place the carrots in a saucepan and add water to cover. Bring to a boil, reduce heat, cover, and simmer for 5 minutes, then drain. Melt the margarine in a skillet at medium temperature, add the onion, and sauté until lightly brown. Combine the drained carrots, rice, and onions, and stir in the remaining ingredients while simmering over low heat for about 10 minutes.

Serves: 6
Heat Scale: Medium

〰〰〰〰〰〰〰

PILAF ON THE PECOS

Surprisingly, Dave grew up eating rice as much as potatoes in Virginia. In the DeWitt family, whoever cooked was exempted from dishwashing, so Dave quickly learned how to make pilaf when he was about eight. It was only natural that he would come up with this one after moving to New Mexico in 1974.

¼ cup olive oil
1   small onion, minced
1   clove garlic, minced
1   cup long-grain rice
2½ cups Rich Vegetable
    Stock (see recipe, p. 5)
1   tablespoon minced fresh
    Mexican oregano (or
    1 teaspoon dried
    oregano)

¼ cup chopped New Mexi-
    can green chiles
3   tablespoons whole piñon
    nuts (or substitute pine
    nuts)

Heat the olive oil in a skillet, add the onion and garlic, and sauté until the onion is soft, about 4 minutes. Add the rice and sauté, stirring constantly, until the rice is golden brown, about 4 to 7 minutes.

Add the stock and bring to a boil. Immediately remove from the heat and stir in the rest of the ingredients.

Transfer the mixture to a Pyrex baking dish and bake, covered, in a 350-degree oven for 45 minutes. For crisper rice, remove the cover for the last 15 minutes of cooking.

Serves: 4 to 6
Heat Scale: Medium

A Good Fixation

There are more than 14,000 species of legumes, the family that includes beans and peas, but only about 22 species are grown for human consumption. This entire family absorbs nitrogen from the air and fixes it in the soil, giving legumes an important role in crop rotation.

HOT GREEN RISOTTO

Now that risotto has been discovered in the U.S., it is not uncommon to see it combined with chiles, as we do in the Southwest.

5 **tablespoons margarine**	1 **cup imported Italian Arborio rice**
4 **cups Rich Vegetable Stock (see recipe, p. 5)**	2 **ounces provolone cheese, grated or diced**
2 **tablespoons olive oil**	¼ **cup freshly grated Parmesan cheese**
5 **cloves garlic, minced**	
1 **cup chopped mild New Mexican green chiles**	

Melt the margarine in a saucepan over medium heat. Meanwhile, in a separate pot, bring the stock to a boil. Add the olive oil and garlic to the margarine and sauté for 3 to 5 minutes or until soft.

Add the green chile and cook another 5 minutes. Stir the rice into the chile mixture and coat thoroughly. Continue cooking until all the liquid evaporates.

Pour about ½ cup of the simmering stock into the rice mixture. Cook and stir until the liquid is evaporated. Continue this process until the rice is creamy and tender.

If you start running out of broth, add some hot water. Stir in the cheeses and continue cooking until they are melted. Serve immediately.

Serves: 4
Heat Scale: Medium

〜〜〜〜〜〜〜〜

YELLOW FESTIVE RICE

Dave and Mary Jane collected this recipe on a trip to Singapore. It is a very colorful rice with curry spice fragrances. *Kunyit* is the Malay word for turmeric; *nasi* is rice.

4   teaspoons ground coriander

2   teaspoons ground cumin

1   teaspoon ground turmeric

1   5-inch piece of ginger, peeled

3   cloves garlic, peeled

10 shallots, peeled

1   cup water

6   tablespoons vegetable oil

6   cups canned low-fat coconut milk (available in Asian markets)

3   cups long-grain rice, washed and drained

4   3-inch stalks lemongrass, including the bulb, chopped

3   small hot red chiles, such as piquins
    Salt to taste
    Fried spring (green) onion rings for garnish

In a food processor, puree together the coriander, cumin, turmeric, ginger, garlic, shallots, and water. Fry this paste in the oil in a saucepan until fragrant, about 5 to 7 minutes. Add the coconut milk and bring to a boil.

Reduce the heat to a simmer. Add the rice, lemongrass, and chiles. Cover and cook until the rice is done, about 40 minutes. Add salt to taste, remove the chiles before serving, and garnish with the fried onion rings.

Serves: 6

Heat Scale: Medium

〰〰〰〰〰〰

TANGY TABULI

This delicious and versatile Middle Eastern dish can also be served as an appetizer or as a salad, take your pick. You can also take your pick from the alternative spellings — *tabbuleh, tabouleh,* or *tabbooli.* It is necessary to hand-chop the ingredients; using a food processor turns this delightful dish into a plate of mush. You want some unevenness and chunkiness to add interest as you scoop it up with romaine leaves. The tabuli can be served on individual plates with a few romaine leaves, or it can be served in a single large mound, surrounded by the romaine — community eating at its best!

1½ **cups bulgur wheat**	⅔ **cup olive oil**
Cold water to cover	⅓ **cup freshly squeezed**
1 **bunch parsley, minced**	**lemon juice**
(about 1½ cups)	**Salt to taste**
1 **bunch green onions,**	1 **large or 2 small heads of**
minced	**romaine lettuce,**
2 **tomatoes, peeled,**	**cleaned, separated, and**
seeded, and finely	**well drained**
chopped	
¾ **cup fresh mint, chopped**	
4 **serrano or jalapeño**	
chiles, seeds and stems	
removed, minced	

Soak the bulgur in enough cold water to cover, for an hour or until soft. Squeeze out the water with your hands or put the bulgur in a fine sieve and press very hard to remove the excess water.

Place the bulgur in a large bowl and gently mix with the parsley, green onions, tomatoes, mint, and chiles.

Drizzle the olive oil over the mixture and, using a large spoon, gently fold it into the mixture. Then pour the lemon juice over this mixture and toss with two spoons to distribute.

Cover and refrigerate overnight to blend the flavors. Serve in a large bowl, surrounded by the romaine leaves.

Serves: 5 as a salad course
Heat Scale: Hot

BODACIOUS BARLEY BAKE

One of the first plants ever eaten by mankind — and the first cultivated crop — Old World barley is mated with New World chile peppers in this recipe, created by Mary Jane.

4 tablespoons oil	½ cup parboiled diced carrots
2 cups chopped green onion, including green tops	½ cup piñons or pine nuts
¼ cup chopped green bell pepper	1 clove garlic, minced
½ cup chopped celery	½ teaspoon marjoram
2 teaspoons New Mexican chile powder (or chipotle chile powder for a smoky taste)	½ teaspoon basil
	2 tablespoons chopped cilantro
1 cup barley (uncooked)	5 cups Rich Vegetable Stock (see recipe, p. 5)

Heat the oil and sauté the onions, onion tops, bell pepper, and celery until slightly limp. Strain the sautéed mixture into a 1½-quart or 2-quart casserole, reserving the oil, and stir in the chile powder.

Add the barley to the same skillet and sauté until it turns golden brown, about 5 minutes. Stir a few times and watch the barley to make sure it doesn't burn. Add the barley to the vegetables in the casserole and then add the carrots, pine nuts, garlic, marjoram, basil, cilantro, and 2 cups of the stock. Cover and bake at 350 degrees for 30 minutes.

Then remove the casserole from the oven and carefully stir in 2 more cups of the stock. Cover and bake for another 30 minutes.

Add the remaining cup of stock, mix well, and bake uncovered for 15 minutes more.

Serves 4 to 6

Heat Scale: Mild

VEGGIE COUSCOUS WITH MEDITERRANEAN HARISSA

North Africa is the home of this dish, which incorporates couscous, a tiny semolina pasta resembling grains of rice, with red-hot chile and spicy vegetables. Our version of *harissa* is much milder than the norm, but that's so you can eat more of it. Total preparation time for this recipe is between 1½ to 2 hours. Plan ahead and find a bit of time to make this fantastic dish — it's worth it!

SPICY VEGGIES

3	tablespoons olive oil	1	cup capers
1	cup snow peas	1	tablespoon minced ginger
2	carrots, chopped	½	teaspoon lemon juice
8	large mushrooms, halved	2	teaspoons brown sugar
1	red onion, coarsely chopped	1	teaspoon ground cinnamon
1	cup minced scallions	½	teaspoon allspice
8	tomatoes, peeled and quartered	½	teaspoon New Mexican red chile powder
1	cup Rich Vegetable Stock (see recipe, p. 5)		

Heat the oil in a large pan until warm but not bubbling. Add the snow peas, carrots, mushrooms, onion, and scallions, and sauté until slightly tender. Add the rest of the ingredients, mixing well, then simmer for about 5 minutes. Set aside.

THE MEDITERRANEAN HARISSA

6	New Mexican red chile pods, such as Chimayo, seeds and stems removed, soaked in water for 15 minutes	9	large Greek olives, pitted and chopped
		3	tablespoons olive oil
		1	teaspoon orange juice

¼ **cup chopped cilantro**

2 **tablespoons chopped capers**

1 **tablespoon minced garlic**

⅓ **cup chopped fresh mint**

½ **teaspoon cumin seeds**

Drain the red chile and puree in a food processor. Place the pureed chile in a mixing bowl along with the olives. Stir in the olive oil and orange juice; add the cilantro and capers, mixing well. Then add the garlic, mint, and cumin seeds. Mix well and set aside.

THE COUSCOUS

25 **to 30 garlic cloves (more or less, depending on your taste for garlic)**

1 **tablespoon olive oil**

4½ **cups Rich Vegetable Stock (see recipe, p. 5)**

3 **tablespoons olive oil**

1 **tablespoon ground cinnamon**

½ **teaspoon ground nutmeg**

¼ **teaspoon saffron**

2¾ **cups couscous**

Preheat the oven to 350 degrees. Coat the garlic cloves with 1 tablespoon olive oil. Place the coated garlic in a small cooking dish and bake for 25 minutes, until a fork can easily pierce a clove. Remove from the oven and set aside.

Place the vegetable stock in a medium saucepan and bring to a boil. Reduce heat and simmer for 2 to 3 minutes. Remove the roasted garlic cloves from their skins and add to the mixture. Stir in the rest of the olive oil and the cinnamon, nutmeg, and saffron. Simmer for 3 minutes and remove from the heat. Stir the couscous into the broth and cover with a lid for 5 minutes. Fluff with a fork, then spoon onto a platter. Place vegetables on top of the couscous and pass around the *harissa* to be spiced to taste.

Serves: 6

Heat Scale: Varies according to amount of the *harissa* added

CURRIED KASHA WITH VEGETABLES

This tasty and unusual main dish has an Indian twist, with the addition of curry powder and the extra punch of chiles. Serve it with a chilled, marinated garlic-cucumber salad. We like to make it in the summer months, when the vegetables are at their peak of freshness.

½ cup fresh shelled peas

1 cup diced carrots

2 cups summer squash, diced

½ cup diced celery

1 cup broccoli florets, broken into small pieces

4 tablespoons olive oil

½ cup diced onion

2 teaspoons curry powder

2 tablespoons whole wheat flour

1 tablespoon guava jelly

1 teaspoon fresh lime juice

1½ cups Rich Vegetable Stock (see recipe, p. 5)

2 serrano chiles, seeds and stems removed, chopped

2 tablespoons canola oil

½ cup kasha

2 cups water

½ teaspoon salt

Steam the peas, carrots, squash, celery, and broccoli until they are *al dente* — that is, cooked but firm. Reserve.

Heat the oil and sauté the onion for 3 minutes. Add the curry powder and flour and mix well. Stir in the guava jelly and the lime juice and simmer for a few seconds.

Add the vegetable stock and the chiles and simmer until the sauce thickens, about 10 minutes. Reserve.

Heat the canola oil, add the kasha, and sauté for 2 minutes. Add the water and the salt and bring to a boil. Then turn the heat down to a simmer, cover, and simmer the kasha for 15 to 20 minutes. Remove from the heat and allow to sit for 10 minutes.

Add the reserved vegetables to the reserved chile-curry stock and heat through. Spoon kasha onto plates, top with the vegetables, and serve.

Serves: 4 to 5

Heat Scale: Medium

DARING DHAL

The Far East meets the Southwest in this recipe. It is easy to make and can be used in a variety of ways: Serve it over rice, use it as a stuffing for parboiled bell peppers, or spoon it into hollowed-out tomatoes. Serve it with a spicy, minted fruit salad.

2   tablespoons vegetable oil

2   cloves minced garlic

1   cup chopped onions

½   teaspoon ground cumin

½   teaspoon ground coriander

2   teaspoons curry powder

2   cups cooked lentils

¾   cup cooked pinto beans or black beans

1   large tomato, peeled, seeded, and coarsely chopped

5   serrano or jalapeño chiles, seeds and stems removed, minced

¼   cup plain yogurt

Heat the oil in a large skillet and sauté the garlic and onion. Add the cumin, coriander, and curry powder and stir until the onion pieces are coated.

Add the cooked lentils, the beans, the chopped tomato, and the chiles.

Stir and heat until the mixture is heated through. Stir in the yogurt.

Serves: 4

Heat Scale: Medium to Hot

For All the Rice in Burma

According to the USA Rice Council, American rice consumption per year is close to 20 pounds per person, compared to just 9 pounds in 1974. By comparison, the French eat but 3½ pounds per year ("The French have never found out how to cook rice." — Elizabeth David). But the United States is still far behind rice-driven nations like Japan (165 pounds per person per year), China (300 pounds), and Burma, now Myanmar (500 pounds). We must remember, though, that in those countries, rice is a staple rather than an option. Interestingly enough, the United States is now the sixth largest rice-producing country in the world.

6

Pungent Pastas and Main Dishes

W hile this book was being written, the third National Health and Nutrition Examination Survey was released by the National Center for Health Statistics. It revealed that cholesterol levels among Americans have dropped so rapidly since 1980 that nearly half of the nation's adults now have healthy blood levels of that substance. The new figures mean that the risk of heart disease has been reduced by as much as 32 percent since 1963.

The drop has occurred because more people than ever are paying attention to their diet, watching their weight, and exercising regularly. Another important factor is reduced consumption of meats and other high-fat, high-cholesterol foodstuffs.

In this chapter, we have assembled a collection of meatless main courses in keeping with the trend toward lowered cholesterol consumption. First come the pastas, which we prepare quite often. In fact, during the summer, Dave seems to live on them for lunch. He goes out to the garden, picks the pesto ingredients, immediately makes a chile-piñon pesto, boils some of his favorite pasta, and has lunch ready in less than 30 minutes.

We begin with the basics: two recipes for hot and spicy pastas, Red Chile Noodles and Jalapeño Pasta. They can be paired with the pasta sauces in Chapter 1 (a double dollop of heat), or served with blander sauces. Penne Pasta with Chile and Sun-Dried Tomatoes, one of Mary Jane's favorites, is delightfully herby, with both basil and Italian parsley; Classic Tomato Spaghetti is simple, light, and spicy. Ravioli With Green Chile-Tofu Filling is surprising because ravioli is not usually stuffed with tofu — but this one works great! Unusual combinations continue with our Habanero Lasagne, in which black olives are marinated with habaneros, and Absolut-ly the Best Pasta, which features spicy vodka. Green and White Spicy Pasta offers the combination of brie, jalapeños, ginger, and shallots; Pasta from Hell — amazingly enough — stars bananas, fruit juices, and habaneros again.

Our next category of main dishes is Meatless Mexican. Removing the meat from some of these dishes, such as Sonoran Enchiladas and Enchiladas Very Verde, was no problem since they didn't have any to begin with! Goat Cheese Poblanos Rellenos with Chipotle Cream, an inspired invention of our friend, chef Rosa Rajkovic, melds three cheeses inside the tastiest chiles of all. A variation is Tofu-Stuffed Poblanos. Meatless fajitas are not only possible but delicious in our Tempting Tempeh Fajitas; another meatless marvel is Todd's Terrific Tofu Adovada, in which tofu is substituted for the usual pork.

Next are our egg entrees, from the Pancho Villa Omelette (our Sunday-brunch favorite) to two spicy frittatas: Spicy Rustic Frittata with Potato Crust and Avocado Feta Frittata, featuring feta cheese combined with avocados and mushrooms.

We have also assembled a collection based on meat substitutes. The Produce Guy's Favorite Burgers substitutes vegetables for beef; Spicy To(o)fu(n) Burgers and Tofu Patties with Spicy Chile Sauce use tofu for the same purpose. Two stir-fry dishes top off the meat substitute entrees: Savory Seitan Simmer with Green Chile and Explosive Tofu-Veggie Stir-Fry.

Finally, there were the meatless main dishes that we simply could not categorize, and thus have labeled "miscellaneous." New-Mex Stroganoff depends on mushrooms for its bulk. Green Chile Polenta with Three Cheeses is a side dish transformed into a main dish; the tomato-avocado-pita (T.A.P.) Sandwich makes a main course for any lunch. We end with a lighter entree, the very different Rosemary Chipotle Crepes.

RED CHILE NOODLES

This homemade pasta is excellent — as it should be, since it comes from Adelina Willem, who manufactures spicy pastas in Las Cruces, New Mexico. She has written on the subject in *Chile Pepper* magazine. To make other chile pastas, simply change the size of the noodles. If you are making them a day ahead of time, store them in the refrigerator.

3   tablespoons hot New Mexican red chile powder

3   cups semolina flour (available in gourmet shops and health food stores)

2   large eggs, beaten lightly

1   tablespoon olive oil

Mix the chile powder and semolina together. Make a well in the middle and place the eggs and olive oil in it.

Mix with your hands and then knead for 10 minutes. Cover the dough and let it sit for ½ hour.

Using a rolling pin (or a pasta machine), roll the dough very thin (1/32 inch or less). Cut into 1½-inch-wide strips.

Cook the noodles in boiling salted water for 1 to 2 minutes — no more. Drain, place on a kitchen towel, and cover with plastic wrap until you are ready to use them in your recipe.

Yield: About ½ to ¾ pound of noodles
Heat Scale: Mild

JALAPEÑO PASTA

From Nanette Blanchard's article on pepper pastas that appeared in *Chile Pepper* magazine comes this additional chile pasta. It has a great fresh chile smell and a golden color with green flecks.

3	**large eggs, at room temperature**
6	**jalapeño chiles, seeds and stems removed, coarsely chopped**

2	**teaspoons olive oil**
2	**cups unbleached flour**
2	**tablespoons water**
	Water or additional flour

Place the eggs, jalapeños, and olive oil in a food processor and puree. Add the flour and continue processing until dough forms a ball.

If the mixture remains crumbly, add the water 1 teaspoon at a time until the dough forms a ball. Knead by hand for 10 minutes to increase the dough's elasticity. Let the dough sit, covered, for 30 minutes.

Using a pasta machine or a rolling pin and a well-floured work area, roll the dough out as thinly as possible (a setting of about 4 on the Atlas hand-cranked pasta machine). Let the sheets of rolled dough dry on the backs of chairs for about 10 minutes before cutting the pasta.

With a sharp knife or a pasta machine, cut the sheets into thin strips to the desired width and hang overnight to dry. To cook home-made pasta, gently immerse in boiling salted water and cook for several minutes or until tender.

Yield: About ¾ pound of pasta
Heat Scale: Medium

PENNE PASTA WITH CHILE AND SUN-DRIED TOMATOES

This flavorful and spicy pasta from Mary Jane is served with a simple green salad, crisp garlic toast, and a chilled dry Italian red wine.

4 tablespoons crushed New Mexican red chiles

½ cup sun-dried tomatoes, cut in slivers

1 cup black olives, cured in oil, pitted and halved

½ cup fresh basil, chopped

½ cup fresh Italian parsley, chopped

1 tablespoon grated lemon peel

3 cloves garlic, minced

½ cup olive oil

2 tablespoons oil from the tomatoes (or substitute olive oil)

2 teaspoons freshly ground black pepper

¾ pound Parmesan cheese, grated

1 pound penne pasta

4 quarts salted water

Combine all the ingredients, except the cheese, pasta, and water, and let sit at room temperature for a couple of hours to blend the flavors.

Cook the pasta in the water until tender but still firm — *al dente*. Drain.

Toss the pasta with the sauce and cheese until well coated, and serve.

Serves: 6
Heat Scale: Medium

〰〰〰〰〰〰〰

CLASSIC TOMATO SPAGHETTI

Unlike the heavy, rich tomato sauces for pasta, this one is simple, light, and spicy — perfect for the warmer months. It can be used as an appetizer or as a light entree. Serve it with herbed *crostini* (crunchy herbed toasts).

1 **pound fresh cherry tomatoes (or ¼ pound sun-
dried cherry tomatoes)**
½ **cup olive oil**
3 **cloves garlic, minced**
2 **teaspoons hot red chile
flakes (such as crushed
piquins)**

Salt and pepper to taste
1 **pound spaghetti**
**Italian parsley leaves for
garnish**
**Grated Pecorino,
Romano, or Parmesan
cheese, for garnish**

Place cherry tomatoes on a baking sheet and bake for 5 minutes at 375 degrees. Remove from the oven and allow to cool for 15 minutes. Cut the tomatoes in half, keeping the seeds and skin.

Heat the olive oil, add the garlic, and sauté for 2 minutes. Then turn the heat up to high, add the tomatoes, and sauté for 5 minutes. Sprinkle with the chile flakes and the salt and pepper.

Cook the spaghetti in boiling salted water until it is *al dente*. Drain and toss with the tomato mixture. Sprinkle the Italian parsley and the cheese on top.

Serves: 4
Heat Scale: Medium

RAVIOLI WITH GREEN CHILE-TOFU FILLING

Ravioli has always been one of our all-time favorite dishes because it presents so many possibilities! One can fill the ravioli with just about anything and create a superb taste that can be savored all at once, or the ravioli can be frozen and served at another meal. This rascally ravioli is a shoo-in for a main dish, but we also like to use it as an appetizer. Set them alongside the spicy dipping sauce of your choice or, better yet, serve different sauces from Chapter 1 with the ravioli to provide the perfect spicy soiree.

THE FILLING

¼ cup chopped New Mexican green chiles

3 cloves garlic, minced

1 4½-ounce can chopped black olives

¾ cup firm (Japanese) tofu, shredded

¼ cup minced onion

¼ cup grated Parmesan cheese

1 tablespoon cilantro

THE RAVIOLI PASTA

1 10-ounce package potsticker wrappers
Cornstarch

1 egg white, beaten
Vegetable oil for frying

Combine all the filling ingredients in a bowl. Chill until ready to use. Next, dust a cookie sheet with cornstarch. Place as many wrappers as will fit on the cookie sheet surface. Brush the wrappers with the beaten egg white. Fill each wrapper with one rounded teaspoon of the filling. Fold each wrapper in half and seal all edges. Place the filled ravioli on a pan in a single layer. Continue the process until all the ravioli are filled and sealed.

Heat the vegetable oil to 375 degrees in a large, deep pot. Fry the ravioli in batches until they are golden brown (about 30 to 45 seconds). Transfer them to paper towels with a slotted spoon to drain off excess oil. Freeze or serve immediately with your favorite sauces.

Yield: 48 ravioli, each 1½-inches square

HABANERO LASAGNE

Give us your bland, give us your vegetarian — we will help! Ours is not a lasagne to be taken lightly; it is filled with the robust flavor of habaneros and black olives — a real taste combination. As you bite into this luscious layered delight, you are temporarily lulled by the garlic-infused sauce; then, all of a sudden, the habanero layer hits your mouth like a cannonball from heaven, then melds with the tastes of the tomato and the vegetables. This recipe requires three days of prior preparation — marinating the olives and peppers, and then some steaming and shuffling on the day of preparation. But making good lasagne has never been easy, or neat.

1 16-ounce can of whole black olives, drained, rinsed, and thinly sliced

3 habanero chiles, seeds and stems removed, minced

½ cup white wine

2 tablespoons olive oil

1 cup chopped onion

¼ cup grated carrots

½ cup finely diced celery

3 cloves garlic, minced

8 ripe tomatoes (2 pounds), peeled, seeded, and chopped (or substitute 1 28-ounce can of whole tomatoes, crushed)

¼ cup sun-dried tomatoes, rehydrated in white wine, then finely chopped

1 8-ounce can of tomato paste (we recommend the best quality you can find)

2 tablespoons dried basil (or 4 tablespoons fresh), chopped

2 teaspoons dried oregano (or 4 tablespoons fresh), chopped

1 bay leaf

¼ cup chopped parsley

½ teaspoon rosemary, crushed

1 teaspoon sugar

1 tablespoon balsamic vinegar

2 cups Rich Vegetable Stock (see recipe, p. 5)

1 pound cooked lasagne noodles

1 or 2 packages frozen artichoke hearts (depending on how big a fan you are), cooked (or substitute 4 fresh zucchini, peeled, sliced horizontally, and steamed for 1 minute)

1 **bunch fresh spinach, cleaned and steamed for 1 minute**	½ **cup grated Parmesan cheese**
1 **pound low-fat ricotta cheese**	1 **cup shredded low-fat mozzarella cheese**

Combine the black olives and the habanero chiles in a glass jar with the white wine. Place the jar in the refrigerator for 3 days and, once a day, turn the jar upside down and shake gently.

In a large, heavy Dutch oven–type casserole, heat the olive oil. Add the onion, carrots, celery, and garlic, and sauté for 2 minutes. Then add the tomatoes, the rehydrated sun-dried tomatoes, and the tomato paste, and mix thoroughly.

Bring the tomato mixture to a low boil and add the basil, oregano, bay leaf, parsley, rosemary, sugar, balsamic vinegar, and 1 cup of the rich stock. (Reserve the second cup of stock to use for thinning, if needed, later on in the cooking.) Cover and simmer for at least 1 hour, stirring occasionally. If the mixture becomes too thick, thin with the reserved stock.

Remove the bay leaf from the tomato sauce and discard. Spread ½ cup of the tomato sauce in a 13-by-9 inch baking dish. Place some cooked lasagne noodles on top of the sauce. Thoroughly drain the olive-habanero mixture, and spread one third of it over the noodles. Top the olive mixture with one third of the sliced artichokes (or zucchini) and one third of the steamed spinach leaves. Mix the three cheeses together and spread one third of this mixture over the spinach.

Pour 1 cup of the tomato sauce over this mixture, and then cover with more lasagne noodles. Repeat the whole process for two more layers, ending with the noodles and topping off with the tomato sauce.

Bake at 350 degrees for 45 minutes. (Or cover and refrigerate and bake later; just allow the dish to reach room temperature before baking.)

Serves: 8 to 10
Heat Scale: Hot

ABSOLUT-LY THE BEST PASTA

This sauce made with Absolut Peppar vodka contains a hint of heat, and tastes so rich it will make your friends think you're Italian!

2   tablespoons margarine
3   cloves garlic, minced
1   teaspoon oregano
1   teaspoon thyme
1   teaspoon rosemary
1   small onion, chopped
1   16-ounce can Italian plum tomatoes, chopped (save liquid)
½   cup Absolut Peppar vodka

½   teaspoon cayenne powder (optional)
¾   cup half-and-half
1   cup freshly grated Parmesan cheese, grated
¾   pound cooked fresh linguini (or substitute 8 ounces dried linguini cooked according to the package's instructions)
    Parsley

In a large skillet, melt the margarine over medium heat. Sauté the garlic, oregano, thyme, rosemary, and onion for about 5 minutes. Add the tomatoes and their liquid and simmer for about 10 minutes, stirring 3 to 4 times. Add the vodka (and the cayenne, if desired) and simmer for about 5 minutes. Add the half-and-half, and half of the Parmesan chese. Simmer for about 4 minutes, or until the sauce thickens lightly. Add the linguini and stir until the sauce coats the pasta. Garnish with parsley and sprinkle the remaining Parmesan on top to taste.

Serves: 4
Heat Scale: Mild without the cayenne, Medium with it

GREEN AND WHITE SPICY PASTA

The unusual combination of ingredients in this recipe makes for a great explosion on the tongue. Other vegetables can be substituted in the sauté — try some zucchini or green beans.

1 tablespoon olive oil

¼ cup minced shallots

3 jalapeño chiles, seeds and stems removed, chopped fine

2 cloves garlic, minced

1 to 1½ cups of Rich Vegetable Stock (see recipe, p. 5)

¾ cup cream or milk

¾ cup dry white wine

¼ teaspoon freshly grated nutmeg

1 teaspoon chopped fresh ginger

2 teaspoons New Mexican red chile powder

½ pound brie, rind removed, diced

2 tablespoons olive oil

½ pound snow peas

1 red bell pepper, seeds removed, cut into ⅛-inch strips

1 yellow bell pepper, seeds removed, cut into ⅛-inch strips

2 yellow summer squashes, peeled and cut into ¼-inch strips

¼ pound mushrooms, cleaned and sliced

1 pound of spinach fettucine

Heat the olive oil in a large heavy skillet and sauté the shallots, chiles, and the garlic for 3 minutes on low heat, taking care not to burn the garlic. Add the stock, the cream or milk, the wine, the nutmeg, the ginger, and the chile powder and bring the mixture to a boil. Lower the heat to a simmer and cook for 20 minutes, stirring occasionally, until the mixture is thickened and reduced by one third.

Add the brie, a few pieces at a time, stirring until the cheese melts. Remove the skillet from the heat and cover to keep warm.

Heat the 2 tablespoons of olive oil in a large skillet and sauté the snow peas, bell peppers, squash, and mushrooms for 3 minutes. Cook the fettucine according to the package directions for *al dente,* drain, and pour into a heated bowl. Add the sautéed vegetables and the chile-wine sauce and gently toss. Serve immediately.

Serves: 6
Heat Scale: Mild

~~~~~~~~~~~~~~~~~~~

PASTA FROM HELL

"This dish is on the outer limits," says Chris Schlesinger, owner of the East Coast Grill in Cambridge, Massachusetts. He featured this pasta in "Equatorial Cuisine," an article he wrote for *Chile Pepper* magazine. The East Coast Grill's Inner Beauty Hot Sauce is available at gourmet shops and by mail order.

2 tablespoons olive oil	3 to 4 tablespoons minced habanero chiles (or ⅓ cup Inner Beauty Hot Sauce, or other habanero-based sauce)
1 yellow onion, diced small	
1 red bell pepper, diced small	
2 bananas, sliced	2 teaspoons margarine
¼ cup pineapple juice	¼ cup grated Parmesan cheese
Juice of 3 oranges	
Juice of 2 limes	1 pound dried fettuccini
¼ cup chopped fresh cilantro	Salt and freshly cracked black pepper to taste

In a large saucepan, heat the oil and sauté the onion and red bell pepper over medium heat for about 4 minutes. Add the bananas and the pineapple and orange juices. Simmer over medium heat for 5 minutes, until the bananas are soft. Remove from the heat. Add lime juice, cilantro, habaneros or Inner Beauty, and 3 tablespoons of the Parmesan cheese, and mix well.

In boiling salted water, cook the fettuccini until *al dente,* about 8 to 10 minutes. Drain and place in a large bowl.

Add the chile mixture and mix well. Season with salt and pepper and garnish with the remaining grated Parmesan.

Serves: 4
Heat Scale: Hot, verging on Extremely Hot

The Invention of Pasta

China, Japan, Korea, Germany, France, and Italy all claim to have invented pasta, and the Italians make their claim more vehemently than all the other countries. Pasta-like dishes existed in Korea prior to the twelfth century A.D., and primitive ravioli were being cooked in Armenia before 1000 A.D. Contrary to popular belief, Marco Polo did not introduce pasta to Italy from China in the thirteenth century. Culinary experts believe that pasta had already sprung up independently in both places, and that noodle-like pastas were made as early as 1500 B.C. — in China.

SONORAN ENCHILADAS

From Antonio Heras-Duran and Cindy Castillo, who took Dave and Mary Jane on a chiltepin tour of Sonora, comes this regional specialty. These enchiladas are not the same as those served north of the border. The main differences are the use of freshly made, thick corn tortillas and the fact that the enchiladas are not baked. We dined on these enchiladas one night in Tucson as they were prepared by Cindy, who is well versed in Sonoran cookcry.

THE SAUCE

15 to 20 chiltepins (or piquins), crushed

15 dried New Mexican red chiles, seeds and stems removed

1 teaspoon salt

Water

3 cloves garlic

1 teaspoon vegetable oil

1 teaspoon flour

In a saucepan, combine the two kinds of chiles, salt, and enough water to cover. Boil for 10 or 15 minutes or until the chiles are quite soft.

Allow the chiles to cool and then puree them in a blender with their water and the garlic. Strain the mixture, mash the pulp through the strainer, and discard the skins.

Heat the oil in a saucepan, add the flour, and brown, taking care that the mixture does not burn. Add the chile puree and boil for 5 or 10 minutes until the sauce has thickened slightly. Set aside and keep warm.

THE TORTILLAS

2 cups *masa harina*

1 egg

1 teaspoon baking powder

1 teaspoon salt

Water

Vegetable oil for deep frying

Mix the first four ingredients together thoroughly, adding enough water to make dough. Using a tortilla press, make the tortillas. Deep-fry each tortilla until it puffs up and turns slightly brown. Remove and drain on paper towels and keep warm.

TO ASSEMBLE AND SERVE

3   to 4 green onions, minced
    (white part only)
2   cups grated *queso blanco*
    or Monterey Jack cheese
    Shredded lettuce

Place a tortilla on each plate and spoon a generous amount of sauce over it. Top with the onions, cheese, and lettuce.

Serves: 4 to 6
Heat Scale: Medium to Hot, depending on the amount of sauce

▼▲▼▲▼▲▼▲▼▲▼▲▼▲▼▲▼▲▼

Great Shapes

There is a seemingly endless variety of pasta shapes, especially from Italy. Estimates of the total number of shapes in Italy range from 350 to 750, but only about 100 are in common use. Beyond the common *vermicelli* ("little worms") are wheels (*ruote*), shells (*lumache* and *conchigilette*), bows (*farfale*), tubes (*penne* and *grosso rigato*), spirals (*tortiglioni*), buttons (*cappelletti*), scalloped ribbons (*mafalde*), and the huge "priest's windpipe" (*strozzapreti*).

▼▲▼▲▼▲▼▲▼▲▼▲▼▲▼▲▼▲▼

ENCHILADAS VERY VERDE

To illustrate the contrasting styles of Mexican enchiladas that we serve, we present a second recipe, which we found in Mexico many years ago. About 20 years ago, we used to make enchiladas with sour cream and then bake them — with mixed results. In Mexico back then, there was no sour cream as we know it, so cooks used a cream-cheese-type cream with excellent results. The beans and the corn add some crunch to the creamy onion filling, all adding up to a "rave" entree. Serve them with Mexicali Rice (see recipe, p. 125) and sliced tomatoes drizzled with olive oil and sprinkled with ground red chile.

8 **ounces softened low-fat cream cheese**	2 **fresh serrano chiles, seeds and stems removed**
½ **cup Rich Vegetable Stock (see recipe, p. 5)**	½ **cup fresh cilantro**
1 **cup low-fat milk**	1 **egg (or egg substitute)**
1 **cup half-and-half (or low-fat milk)**	½ **teaspoon salt (optional)**
1 **cup finely chopped onions**	¼ **teaspoon freshly ground black pepper**
1½ **cups chopped New Mexican green chiles (or 6 poblano chiles, roasted, peeled, seeds and stems removed, chopped)**	¼ **cup vegetable oil**
	12 **corn tortillas**
	1½ **cups cooked pinto beans or black beans, 2 tablespoons per tortilla**
1 **10-ounce jar green taco sauce (see note at end of recipe)**	1¼ **cups slightly cooked whole-kernel corn**

In a large mixing bowl, beat the cream cheese until it is smooth, adding ¼ cup of the stock and ¼ cup of the milk. Beat until the mixture is thoroughly blended. Add the chopped onions and mix. Set aside.

Place in a blender the green chiles, the green taco sauce, the serrano chiles, the cilantro, the egg, the salt (if desired), the black pepper, the remaining stock, and the remaining milk (and/or half-and-half). Blend on high speed for 15 seconds. Pour the puree into a bowl.

In a heavy, small skillet, heat 2 tablespoons of the oil. When the oil sizzles (flick a drop of water into the oil), quickly fry the tortillas, one at a time, in the oil, about 5 seconds on each side. You just want to soften them, not fry the life out of them. Drain them on layers of paper towels.

To assemble in a large glass casserole dish (9 by 13 inches): Dip a tortilla into the puree, drain for a second, and place in the glass pan. (This procedure is messy.) Spread the tortilla with some of the cream cheese–onion mix and add 2 tablespoons of beans and 1 tablespoon of the whole-kernel corn. Roll up tightly, and place the filled tortilla to one side of the glass casserole, seam side down. Fill the remaining tortillas and place in the pan. Pour the remaining sauce over the filled tortillas.

Bake in a 350-degree oven for 15 to 20 minutes.

Serves: 6 (2 filled tortillas per person)
Heat Scale: Medium

Note: We prefer La Victoria Brand Green Taco Sauce because it has a lot of the tomatillo taste that we like. However, other brands may be just as good — just check the ingredients to make sure that there is a fair amount of tomatillos in the list of ingredients.

〰〰〰〰〰〰〰〰

GOAT CHEESE POBLANOS RELLENOS WITH CHIPOTLE CREAM

Chef Rosa Rajkovic of the Monte Vista Fire Station restaurant in Albuquerque created these cheese-infused stuffed peppers, on which we have dined many times. She says that because of the varying heat scales of poblanos (they are usually quite mild), preparing this recipe is "culinary roulette." However, the cheese does cut the heat of any renegade poblanos.

CHIPOTLE CREAM

½ **cup sour cream**
¼ **cup chevre (goat cheese)**
1 **small chipotle chile (if dry, soak it in water first to soften)**

Half-and-half or heavy cream
1 **tablespoon cilantro, chopped fine**

Process or blend together the sour cream, goat cheese, and chipotle until very smooth. Add enough half-and-half or cream for a consistency that can be poured. Add the cilantro and process for a few seconds longer. Pour the cream into a squeeze bottle, but make sure the cilantro is fine enough that it doesn't clog the opening.

Yield: About 1 cup

RELLENOS

6 **large poblano chiles**
½ **pound chevre (goat cheese)**
⅓ **pound low-fat cream cheese**
¼ **pound cambozola or sago bleu cheese**

2 **eggs, beaten**
1 **cup blue corn meal**
½ **cup canola or vegetable oil**
Chipotle Cream

Roast the poblanos on a grill, over gas burners, or under a broiler until the skins blister and blacken. Remove the peppers from the heat, place them in a bowl, and cover tightly with plastic wrap. Allow the peppers to cool completely. Peel the peppers; carefully slit each one along one side and remove the seeds. Leave the stem intact.

Mix or process the three cheeses together and pipe (using a pastry bag with a plain tip or coupler) or spoon the mixture into the cavities of the peppers. Refrigerate until you are ready to assemble the final dish. (*Tip:* chilling the rellenos until they are very cold will help the blue corn coating stay crisp after the rellenos are sautéed.)

Right before serving, assemble the eggs and blue corn meal in two separate shallow bowls. Heat the oil in a large skillet over medium-low heat. Dip the rellenos into the egg mixture first and then into the blue corn meal. Sauté the rellenos until lightly browned, turning each one 3 times in the hot oil to ensure even crisping. Drain on double-thickness paper toweling.

Place the rellenos in shallow bowls and artistically drizzle the Chipotle Cream over them.

Serves: 6

Heat Scale: Varies with the poblanos, but probably Mild

TOFU-STUFFED POBLANOS

This superb recipe, another variation on stuffed chiles, was given to us by chef Todd Sanson, the day chef at the El Nido Restaurant in Santa Fe. Todd spends his days creating fine dishes at the restaurant, and his weekends as a caterer to various movie stars who now live in "The City Different."

8	large poblano chiles, roasted and peeled	1	cup tofu, drained and sautéed in a robust oil (peanut or sesame)
1	cup golden raisins (or substitute regular raisins or currants)	1	cup shredded Monterey Jack cheese
½	cup toasted piñons (or pumpkin seeds or sunflower seeds)	2	cups soft goat cheese or feta cheese
1	cup cooked yellow corn kernels		

Cut a slit in the side of each poblano and remove the seeds. Mix together all the ingredients, except the poblanos, in a large bowl. Stuff this mixture into the poblanos.

Place the stuffed chiles on a greased cookie sheet. At the slit in each poblano, place a teaspoon or so of shredded cheese. This cheese will melt and allow the chile to hold together better in the oven.

Heat the oven to 375 degrees and bake the poblanos for 15 to 20 minutes, or until the cheese is bubbling. Place the chiles on a heated plate and cover with Quick Red Chile Mole Sauce (see recipe, p. 21).

Serves: 4
Heat Scale: Medium

~~~~~~~~~~~

TEMPTING TEMPEH FAJITAS

This spicy recipe comes from our friend Jeanette DeAnda, who is an excellent creative chef and caterer. If you don't know what to make for dinner some night, call Jeanette; she'll give you 20 ideas off the top of her head! This recipe is also great when it is used as a stuffing for burritos. Serve this tempeh dish with flour tortillas and garnishes such as salsa, fresh slices of lime, guacamole, tomatoes, and green onions. The ingredients of choice can be wrapped up in the tortilla and eaten like a sandwich.

2   teaspoons brown sugar
¼   cup water
¼   cup tamari sauce
4   jalapeño chiles, seeds and stems removed, thinly sliced
2   cloves garlic, minced
    Juice from 2 limes
1   pound tempeh, sliced into thin strips

½   green bell pepper, seeds removed, cut in thin strips, lengthwise
½   red bell pepper, seeds removed, cut in thin strips, lengthwise
½   yellow onion, sliced
4   flour tortillas

In an ovenproof casserole dish, mix the brown sugar, water, tamari, chiles, garlic, and lime juice, and mix in the sliced tempeh. Marinate the mixture for at least 45 minutes.

Add the bell pepper and the onion to the tempeh mixture and mix gently. Bake the tempeh at 350 degrees for 15 minutes, covered. Remove the cover and broil for 3 to 5 minutes. Spoon the tempeh into the tortillas and serve sizzling hot.

Serves: 4
Heat Scale: Medium

Fiery Foods: Fad or Trend? Part 4

George Blooston, writing in *Savvy* magazine in 1989, asked, "Is this just another gastronomic fad, destined to shrivel like so many sun-dried tomatoes? If past performance is any guide, the answer is no. Serrano, poblano, habanero, and cayenne peppers, which are native to South America, are the culinary equivalent of kudzu. They take hold of a cuisine and don't let go. The ancients ate them and, when the time came, showed them to Columbus, who, you'll recall, set sail in search of a shortcut to India and its enticing spices. It is estimated that today at least three-fourths of the human race takes its meals chile-hot."

TODD'S TERRIFIC TOFU ADOVADA

This is a tasty tofu recipe from chef Todd Sanson. He says, "This is a great way to still have a traditionally flavored New Mexican dish with the heat, but without the meat." This dish can be served with red chile sauce, served in a bowl, or used as a filling in flour tortillas for burritos. Serve it with a bowl of pinto beans or black beans and a big green salad.

4 pounds (4 packages) of firm tofu

6 tablespoons flavored oil for sautéing (peanut, sesame, or avocado)

2 medium onions, chopped

3 cloves garlic, minced

1 teaspoon oregano

2 teaspoons crushed coriander seed

2 tablespoons honey

⅓ cup New Mexican red chile powder

¼ cup ancho chile powder

1 tablespoon chile caribe (crushed hot red chiles, such as piquin or santaka)

3 tablespoons sherry vinegar or rice wine

¼ cup toasted pumpkin seeds

1 tablespoon ground cinnamon

2 cups Rich Vegetable Stock (see recipe, p. 5)
   Salt to taste

Place several layers of paper towels on a cookie sheet. Slice the tofu in half lengthwise and place the halves on the towels. Cover the tofu with several more layers of paper towels and another cookie sheet. Then put some heavy objects on the sheet to weight down the tofu; heavy canned goods will work, and Todd suggests using your thick French cookbooks. Allow the tofu to sit for 20 minutes. Then cut it into ½-inch cubes.

Heat the oil in a large skillet, add the cubed tofu, and sauté until golden brown. Set aside.

Pour 1 cup of stock into a blender and add the rest of the ingredients, except for the remaining stock. Puree for a few seconds, add the stock, and blend again. Pour into a large bowl and gently mix in the sautéed tofu.

Refrigerate for 1 to 2 hours. Then take the mixture out of the refrigerator and allow it to stand for 10 minutes.

Pour the mixture into a deep saucepan and bring to a boil. Turn the heat down and simmer for one hour. Adjust seasonings and serve.

Serves: 6 to 8
Heat Scale: Hot

∿∿∿∿∿∿∿∿∿∿

PANCHO VILLA OMELETTE

We try to be good and cut down on eggs, but on weekends we cheat with this great brunch dish. It tends to change, according to what's available in the refrigerator, but the basic green chile and low-fat cream cheese are the two constants. If you have leftover vegetables, olives, and so on, spread them on the omelette before it is folded over. We like to serve it topped with Ketchup with a Kick (see recipe, p. 8) and accompanied by spicy El Rancho Potatoes (see recipe, p. 184).

2 tablespoons margarine
3 eggs (or egg substitute)
3 tablespoons water
¼ cup low-fat cream cheese, softened

½ cup chopped New Mexican green chiles

In a small skillet, melt the margarine. Whisk the eggs and water together briskly, and carefully pour the mixture into the sizzling margarine. Turn the heat down to low; using a fork, lift the edges of the omelette to allow the uncooked egg to run underneath. When most of the egg mixture has run off the top, dot the softened cream cheese over the top and follow with the green chile. Carefully fold one half of the omelette over onto the other half, allowing some of the uncooked mixture to ooze out and cook. Cut the omelette in half, again allowing anything uncooked to run out and cook. Serve immediately.

Serves: 2
Heat Scale: Medium

ᴧᴧᴧᴧᴧᴧᴧᴧᴧᴧ

SPICY RUSTIC FRITTATA
WITH POTATO CRUST

Many thanks to Donald Downes for this great entree. When it comes to great food, Donald knows. He is currently a restaurant critic for *Phoenix Magazine* and a graduate of the Scottsdale Culinary Institute. In addition, he has worked professionally at The Boulders. The ingredients for this recipe are staples that most of us have in our kitchens; Donald raises them to gourmet status in this frittata recipe.

1	egg, plus 2 egg whites
¼	teaspoon salt
	Freshly ground black pepper
3½	tablespoons canola oil
2	medium potatoes, grated and rinsed 3 times and squeezed dry (see note at end of recipe)
1	cup sliced mushrooms
2	cloves garlic, minced
½	teaspoon dried thyme (or 1½ teaspoons fresh thyme)
3	green onions, chopped
2	jalapeño chiles, seeds and stems removed, minced
1	small red bell pepper, seeds removed, diced
½	cup frozen corn kernels, thawed and rinsed
1	teaspoon fresh lemon juice
2	tablespoons grated Parmesan cheese
1	cup grated Monterey Jack cheese
2	to 3 tablespoons chopped cilantro, for garnish

In a bowl, whisk together the egg and the egg whites, ⅛ teaspoon of the salt, a small amount of black pepper (one turn of the grinder), and ½ tablespoon of canola oil. Set the mixture aside.

Heat 2 tablespoons of canola oil in a large non-stick skillet over medium-high heat. Add the potatoes to the hot oil and cook until they are crisp and browned, stirring as needed.

In another non-stick skillet, heat the remaining tablespoon of oil. Add the mushrooms, garlic, thyme, green onions, jalapeño chile, and the red pepper. Sauté for 2 to 3 minutes and then add the corn, the remaining ⅛ teaspoon of salt, and the lemon juice. Cook the mixture, stirring, until the vegetables are tender and all of the liquid has evaporated, about 5 minutes. Stir in the Parmesan cheese.

Reduce the heat under the potatoes to low and pour in the egg mixture. Cook until it begins to set, about 1 minute. Spread the vegetable mixture evenly over the eggs. Sprinkle the Jack cheese evenly over the top and cover. Cook just until the cheese melts. Slide the cooked frittata onto a warm serving plate, garnish with the cilantro, and cut it into wedges. Serve immediately.

Serves: 4 to 6
Heat Scale: Medium

Note: If the potatoes haven't been rinsed thoroughly in cold water, the result will be a gooey, sticky mess in your skillet.

〜〜〜〜〜〜〜〜〜

AVOCADO FETA FRITTATA

Our second frittata, from Melissa, is quite different. If you're an avocado fan, you won't want to miss this dish. Serve it with a chilled fruit salad that has been marinated with freshly ground ginger or a tossed salad of greens, sliced red onions, and sections of oranges and grapefruit, topped with a sprinkle of champagne vinegar and olive oil.

½ **large ripe avocado, cut into 1-inch squares**
1 **tomato, chopped**
1 **teaspoon lime juice**
   Pinch of salt
1 **ounce feta cheese, crumbled**
¼ **teaspoon rosemary**

4 **black olives, minced**
4 **fresh mushrooms, washed and sliced**
3 **eggs (or egg substitute)**
½ **teaspoon cayenne powder**
1½ **teaspoons olive oil**

Preheat the broiler of your oven. Combine the avocado and tomato with the lime juice and the salt. Add the feta, rosemary, olives, and mushrooms; stir gently. In another bowl, whisk the eggs and cayenne powder together.

Using an oven-safe skillet, warm the oil over medium-high heat. When the oil is bubbling but not smoking, add the eggs. Cook the eggs briefly, stirring once, until the bottom is set and the top is still runny. Remove from the heat and spread the feta-avocado mixture evenly over the eggs. With the mixture still in the skillet, place under the broiler until the frittata is set and the edges are golden brown.

Serves: 2
Heat Scale: Mild

THE PRODUCE GUY'S FAVORITE BURGERS

Okay, prepare yourself for totally vegetarian burgers. Sure, they're good for you, but they taste good, too. And just think — none of these vegetables were fed any hormones!

1½ cups finely chopped walnuts

¼ cup chopped green bell pepper

¼ cup chopped red bell pepper

½ cup chopped New Mexican green chiles

3 cloves garlic, minced

4 scallions, chopped

¼ cup chopped carrots

1¼ cups thawed frozen spinach, finely chopped

1¼ cups whole wheat bread crumbs

1 tablespoon tarragon, chopped

2 tablespoons chopped celery

¼ cup mayonnaise

¼ teaspoon black pepper

2 tablespoons margarine

Combine all the ingredients, except the margarine, in a large bowl. Shape into 6 patties. Melt the margarine in a large pan and sauté the patties, browning on both sides, until cooked, about 8 to 10 minutes total.

Serves: 6
Heat Scale: Medium

∿∿∿∿∿∿∿

SPICY TO(O)FU(N) BURGERS

The next burger step is to try tofu. Tofu burgers are great fun to cook because it is such a surprise to see how much people enjoy them — especially meat-eaters, who occasionally start out a bit skeptical but are quickly converted.

1 **pound firm tofu**	2 **cups mashed potatoes**
2 **teaspoons New Mexican red chile powder**	6 **shallots, chopped**
½ **teaspoon dill**	½ **cup bread crumbs**
⅓ **cup Monterey Jack cheese, grated**	2 **tablespoons margarine**

Place the tofu in a colander and drain thoroughly. When completely drained, pat dry with paper towels, chop into small pieces, and place it in a bowl.

In the same bowl with the tofu, combine the red chile powder, dill, cheese, potatoes, and shallots. Mix well and shape into 6 patties. Gently coat each burger with bread crumbs.

In a large skillet, melt the margarine over medium heat and cook the patties for about 5 minutes on each side.

Serves: 6
Heat Scale: Mild

∿∿∿∿∿∿∿∿∿∿∿∿

TOFU PATTIES WITH SPICY CHILE SAUCE

Even though the list of ingredients seems to go on forever, this dish is very easy to make and will bring great reviews from your family or guests. Our friend, Jeanette DeAnda, is the creator of this tongue-tingling entree.

¼ **cup tamari sauce**	1 **pound firm tofu, rinsed, drained, carefully towel-squeezed, and sliced into ½-inch patties**
½ **cup water**	
1 **tablespoon brown sugar**	
½ **teaspoon grated fresh ginger**	1 **cup unbleached flour**
2 **cloves garlic, minced**	

1 tablespoon New Mexican red chile powder	1 tablespoon Chile-Infused Oil (see recipe, p. 6)
½ cup peanut oil	

Mix the first five ingredients together and add the sliced tofu. Marinate for 1 hour.

Mix the peanut oil and chile oil together. Mix the flour and chile together, lightly flour the tofu patties, and fry them in the oil until lightly browned. Reserve 2 tablespoons of the oil.

SPICY CHILE SAUCE

2 tablespoons reserved peanut-chile oil	1 teaspoon freshly grated ginger
2 cloves garlic, minced	3 tablespoons tamari sauce
2 green onions, chopped	¼ cup water
3 serrano chiles, seeds and stems removed, minced	¼ cup dry sherry
1 tablespoon freshly squeezed lemon juice	1 tablespoon chopped fresh cilantro

Heat the reserved 2 tablespoons of peanut-chile oil in a skillet. Add the garlic, onions, and chiles, and fry for 2 to 3 minutes. Add the remaining ingredients, except the cilantro, and simmer for 5 minutes. Add the cilantro and stir. Serve the sauce with the patties over mung bean noodles or rice.

Serves: 4

Heat Scale: Medium

SAVORY SEITAN SIMMER WITH GREEN CHILE

This dish really tastes like beef! And of course we added a bit of heat to make it complete! Serve it with rice pilaf.

1 tablespoon vegetable oil	8 ounces seitan, cut into thin rectangles
2 medium onions, thinly sliced	¼ cup white wine
¼ cup chopped New Mexican green chiles	½ cup fresh thyme, chopped
2 cups mushrooms, thinly sliced	¼ cup tahini
	1 teaspoon prepared Dijon-style mustard

Place the oil in a pan and sauté the onions, chile, and mushrooms over low heat for 20 minutes. Add the seitan and white wine and simmer until the seitan is heated completely. Take the mixture off the heat and gently stir in the thyme, tahini, and mustard. Serve immediately over rice.

Serves: 4

Heat Scale: Mild

∿∿∿∿∿∿∿∿∿∿∿∿

EXPLOSIVE TOFU-VEGGIE STIR-FRY

Tofu, because of its absorbent nature, tends to hold a lot of flavors well. In this stir-fry dish, the tofu combines with fresh vegetables and three kinds of peppers for the perfect one-two-three punch!

8 ounces of regular tofu, drained and cut into ½-inch cubes	2 teaspoons red chile paste (available at Asian markets)
¼ cup Rich Vegetable Stock (see recipe, p. 5)	2 teaspoons brown sugar
1 teaspoon cornstarch	1 tablespoon soy sauce
	1 teaspoon peanut oil

4   tablespoons safflower oil
3   cups mushrooms,
    stemmed and sliced
1   tablespoon peeled and
    minced fresh ginger
2   cloves garlic, minced

2   tablespoons minced
    jalapeño chile
½   cup sliced red bell pepper
½   cup sliced scallions
    Freshly cooked rice

Place a double layer of paper towels in a colander. Place the tofu cubes on the towels to drain for at least 25 minutes. Combine the vegetable broth and cornstarch in a bowl until the cornstarch is dissolved. Whisk in the chile paste, brown sugar, soy sauce, and peanut oil. Set the mixture aside.

Heat two tablespoons of the safflower oil in a wok (or a large pan) over high heat. Add the tofu and stir-fry until it is light brown. Remove the tofu from the wok and place on a plate, using a slotted spoon. Put the rest of the safflower oil in the wok, and continue to heat on high. Add the mushrooms first, and stir-fry for about 5 minutes. Next, add the rest of the ingredients, including the tofu, and stir-fry for about for 1 minute. Last, stir the broth-cornstarch mixture into the wok and bring to a boil. Divide the rice onto plates and top with tofu-vegetable stir-fry.

Serves: 4
Heat Scale: Medium

〜〜〜〜〜〜〜

NEW-MEX STROGANOFF

This is an entree that we like to serve in the cooler months. It is rich, filling, and mouth-watering. The two types of mushrooms add body and flavoring to the sauce. Serve over hot wide noodles, with a chilled marinated salad of garlic, vinegar, and cucumbers, or a hot salad of spicy sweet-sour red cabbage. Some kind of crunchy rolls would be nice, to sop up all the sauces.

3 tablespoons good olive oil

1 onion, diced

1 pound button mushrooms, washed and sliced

⅛ ounce dried porcini mushrooms, rehydrated, rinsed, and diced

3 tablespoons flour

¼ cup dry white wine

¾ cup Rich Vegetable Stock (see recipe, p. 5)

1 clove garlic, minced

½ teaspoon thyme

½ teaspoon dried basil

2 tablespoons hot Hungarian paprika (Szeged brand preferred)

2 teaspoons New Mexican red chile powder

3 tablespoons minced fresh parsley

2 tablespoons minced fresh chives

2 cups low-fat sour cream (or a mix of sour cream and plain yogurt)

Salt and pepper to taste

12 to 16 ounces wide noodles, cooked

Heat the olive oil in a large skillet, add the onion, and sauté for a minute. Add all the mushrooms and let the mixture sauté for a minute or two until only some of the mushroom juice is left. Sprinkle the mixture with the flour and toss lightly until the vegetables are evenly coated.

Add the wine and the stock, stirring until the mixture starts to thicken. Reduce the heat to a simmer and add the garlic, thyme, basil, paprika, and chile powder. Cover and let the mixture simmer for about 15 minutes to blend the flavors. Check to see that there is enough liquid in the skillet; if more is needed, thin with more stock or wine.

Add the parsley, the chives, and the sour cream, stirring thoroughly. Do not let the mixture boil. Add salt and pepper to taste.

Serve over the wide boiled noodles and garnish with more parsley if desired. If you have enough Rich Vegetable Stock, try boiling the noodles (either white or spinach) in it for a richer flavor.

Serves: 4 to 5
Heat Scale: Mild

GREEN CHILE POLENTA
WITH THREE CHEESES

We think this recipe is especially wonderful — but then it's hard to go wrong any time you combine fresh green chiles and three cheeses.

4 cups Rich Vegetable Stock (see recipe, p. 5)	1 cup shredded jalapeño cheese
1½ cups cornmeal	1 cup shredded Fontina cheexe
3 New Mexican green chiles, roasted, peeled, seeds and stems removed, chopped (or ½ cup chopped New Mexican green chiles)	½ cup grated Parmesan cheese
	½ cup half-and-half

Preheat the oven to 350 degrees. In a saucepan, heat 2 cups of the stock until it boils. In a mixing bowl, combine the remaining 2 cups of the broth and the polenta, stirring until smooth. Pour the polenta mixture into the boiling broth. Cook over medium heat for about 10 minutes, or until the polenta clings to the side of the pan.

Lightly grease a shallow 6-cup casserole dish. Pour half of the polenta into the casserole dish. Smooth out the batter with a spatula, then sprinkle half of the green chile and half of each of the cheeses evenly over the mixture. Pour half-and-half over the batter. Next, spoon the remaining polenta over the top of the prepared casserole. Sprinkle with the rest of the chile and top with the remaining cheese. Bake until the casserole is bubbly, about 25 minutes. Let cool for 10 to 15 minutes at room temperature before serving.

Serves: 4
Heat Scale: Medium

T.A.P. SANDWICH

Dagwood would definitely make a beeline for this sandwich, which incorporates tomatoes, avocados, and pita — the T.A.P.

1	cup plain non-fat yogurt	2	tomatoes, chopped fine
2	tablespoons tahini	1	avocado, peeled, seeded, halved, and cut into crescent shapes
2	teaspoons lime juice		
2	teaspoons paprika	½	cup chopped New Mexican chiles
1	shallot, minced		
4	pita breads, sliced in half and opened into pockets	¼	cup chopped mint
8	ounces tofu, drained and cut into sandwich-size slices	8	sprigs parsley

In a small bowl, combine the yogurt, tahini, lime juice, paprika, and shallot. Mix well and set aside.

Open each pita pocket. Separate the tofu into 8 equal portions. Insert 1 portion of tofu in each pocket, along with equal parts of tomato, avocado, chile, and mint. Spoon 2 teaspoons of tahini sauce into each pocket. Garnish with parsley.

Yield: 8 half-pita sandwiches
Heat Scale: Medium

~~~~~~~~~~

ROSEMARY CHIPOTLE CREPES

This fragrant, smoky, and elegant dish turns any brunch into something special. Serve the crepes with a salad from Chapter 3 and a soup from Chapter 4.

2 teaspoons margarine
1 egg
1 chipotle chile in adobo
   sauce, pureed
¼ teaspoon salt

⅛ teaspoon pepper
¾ cup milk
½ cup flour
1 teaspoon rosemary

Melt the margarine. Pour it into a bowl and add the, egg, chipotle, salt, pepper, and milk. Add the flour to the batter slowly, whisking continually. Add the rosemary and more margarine or milk (if needed) until the mixture reaches the consistency of heavy cream. Let the batter sit for 20 minutes.

Heat a small non-stick crepe pan over medium heat. Lightly coat the pan with a non-stick cooking spray. Pour 3 tablespoons of the batter into the pan, turning the pan so that the batter covers the bottom evenly. Turn the crepe gently when the edges look dry and begin to turn up slightly, about 30 seconds. Repeat with the remaining batter. Stack crepes between waxed paper.

Yield: 8 crepes (varies depending on the size of the crepe pan)
Heat Scale: Medium

▼▲▼▲▼▲▼▲▼▲▼▲▼▲▼▲▼▲▼▲▼▲▼

Capsaicin Conquers Clusters

The chemical commonly called capsaicin not only gives chile peppers their bite, but also may cure cluster headaches, the most excruciating form of headache known. This neurovascular disease, an intense and debilitating pain around one eye, strikes an estimated 1 percent of the world's population.

A team of reseachers at the University of Florence, Italy, led by Dr. Bruno M. Fusco, treated cluster headache sufferers for several days with a nasal spray containing capsaicin. During a 60-day follow-up period, 11 of the 16 people treated reported a complete cessation of headaches. Two others reported a 50-percent reduction.

The researchers indicated that capsaicin stimulates — then blocks — a class of sensory nerve cells responsible for recognizing and then transmitting pain. One researcher observed that capsaicin "depletes the nerve endings of the chemicals which induce pain." Repeated sprayings, until the burn of the capsaicin could no longer be felt, deadened the nerves and blocked the transmission of cluster-headache pain signals to the brain.

▼▲▼▲▼▲▼▲▼▲▼▲▼▲▼▲▼▲▼▲▼▲▼

Garden
and Grill

Now it's time to harvest our gardens and adjourn to the kitchen — or to the patio, as the case may be. Before we get to the recipes, a few comments about grilling are in order. First, we do not like charcoal and only use it in emergencies. The reason is simple: good charcoal, which used to be partially combusted chunks of wood, is very difficult to find. Instead, charcoal these days consists of uniform briquets made from a slurry that consists of, among other things, scrap plywood. We believe this charcoal, and the starter fluids used to ignite it, impart a chemical flavoring to foods. Therefore, we grill over aromatic hardwoods such as oak, apple, and — our favorite — pecan.

Grilling over wood rather than charcoal is well worth the effort, though more difficult. In the first place, the woods burn hot and then die quickly, which means that timing is critical. However, since most vegetables don't take nearly as long to grill as do meats, this dying out of the fire is not usually a problem — just adjust the height of the grill over the coals.

It is interesting to look at the barbecue books published in the '50s and '60s and compare them to the ones published now. The main difference is that the older books only occasionally have recipes for grilling vegetables. But the later books have corrected that lapse, and now grilled-vegetable recipes are common.

But before we get to the grilling recipes in this book, we present nearly every way to cook hot and spicy vegetables that we can think of, in addition to what we've already covered. First are the baked vegetables, with Chiles Rellenos Casserole leading the list. We've already shown cooks how to stuff poblano chiles, and this recipe is an easier method, featuring the New Mexican long green chiles. Squash is the star of our two versions of calabacitas, Spanish Calabacitas (with soy cheese), and Classic Calabacitas (with cheddar cheese). Spicy Baked Beets with Ginger and Citrus also contains horseradish and red chile powder, which makes for a fascinating combination of flavors. Multi-National Spicy Eggplant Bake is another such combination — this time with mint, rice, and green chile.

Mary Jane provides a surprise with the decidedly different Spicy Sweet Potatoes Anna; onions, chard, and chiles collide in Savory Swiss Chard Pie. In Classic Cilantro Ratatouille, the dish is first sautéed, then baked to blend the flavors of cilantro and 10 other vegetables!

Our fried vegetables are next, starting with Balkan Ajvar, an eggplant-pepper spread from *Chile Pepper* contributing editor Sharon Hudgins. El Rancho Potatoes, another Sunday-brunch favorite, is often served with the Pancho Villa Omelette from Chapter 6. Yapingachos, a South American potato specialty, and Spicy Indian Cabbage and Coconut complete our fried veggies. Braised vegetables include Paprika Mushrooms (another great one from Sharon Hudgins), Melissa's Green Beans à la Simon and Garfunkel, and Braised Broccoli, which should never be overcooked.

Last but not least, we arrive at the grill. Blackened Italian Peppers is ridiculously simple and very tasty. So is Ears and Bells Over the Fire, which eventually becomes a salad. Sealing vegetables in foil and then grilling them is the technique for Grilled Oriental Vegetables, and Grilled Summer Squash with Lemon Garlic Marinade is an excellent way to reduce those bumper crops of zucchini and yellow squash.

CHILES RELLENOS CASSEROLE

From *Chile Pepper* food editor Nancy Gerlach comes a simplified version of stuffed chiles. She comments, "This method of preparing chiles rellenos is easier than the traditional method, though equally delicious. If fresh chiles are not available, canned may be substituted, but be sure to rinse them well."

2 tablespoons vegetable oil	1 cup grated cheddar cheese
1 small onion, chopped	3 eggs
2 cloves garlic, minced	¼ cup flour
8 New Mexican green chiles, roasted, peeled, stems removed	¾ cup milk
½ pound Monterey Jack cheese, cut in strips	¼ teaspoon salt

Sauté the onion and garlic in the oil until soft, about 4 minutes. Remove from the heat and reserve.

Cut a slit down the side of each chile and carefully remove the seeds. Gently stuff each chile with the cheese strips. Lay the chiles side by side in a greased 9-by-13-inch casserole dish. Sprinkle them with the cheddar cheese.

Beat the eggs with the flour until smooth. Add the milk, salt, and onion mixture and mix well. Carefully pour this mixture over the chiles.

Bake, uncovered, for 35 minutes at 350 degrees or until a knife inserted in the custard top comes out clean and the casserole is lightly browned. Remove from the oven and let the casserole cool for 5 to 10 minutes before cutting it with a very sharp knife.

Serves: 4 to 6
Heat Scale: Medium

SPANISH CALABACITAS

Adam's Table is an outstanding vegetarian restaurant in Albuquerque, New Mexico. We coaxed this recipe from the restaurant's head cook Ignacio Griego, Sr., who professes to be a closet vegetarian. He still eats meat occasionally, but for the most part he dines on great veggie dishes like this one.

1	teaspoon corn oil	1½	tablespoons garlic, minced
6	zucchinis, chopped	1½	teaspoons salt
6	green bell peppers, seeds removed, chopped	1½	cups soy cheese, grated
6	onions, cut into ½-inch-long strips	¾	cup scallions, chopped
4	cups corn kernels, drained	¾	cup New Mexican green chiles, chopped
1½	tablespoons onion powder		

Preheat the oven to 375 degrees. Sauté the zucchinis, bell peppers, onions, and corn together in a minimum of corn oil until the vegetables are cooked but still firm. Place the sautéed vegetables in a glass baking dish. Stir in the onion powder, garlic, and salt. Top with soy cheese, scallions, and chile. Bake for 15 minutes at 375 degrees.

Serves: 12
Heat Scale: Medium

∿∿∿∿∿∿∿∿∿∿

CLASSIC CALABACITAS

Calabacitas have many variations, and we frequently cook this particular version that was given to us by our friend, Clara Sanchez. If you have a small garden, you can supply most of the ingredients to provide that extra taste of freshness. Serve this with spicy grilled burgers from Chapter 6 and a big green salad — from your garden, is possible.

2   tablespoons olive oil or margarine

½   cup diced onion

1   clove garlic, minced

2   medium zucchinis, washed, cut in quarters horizontally, and cut into ½-inch cubes

1   ear cooked fresh corn, cut off the cob

¼   cup chopped New Mexican green chile

¼   cup grated cheddar cheese

2   to 4 tablespoons milk

2   tablespoons bread crumbs

Heat the olive oil in an ovenproof medium skillet. Sauté the onion for 1 minute, then add the garlic and the zucchinis and sauté for 1 minute. Add the corn and the green chile and mix gently. Add the cheese and 2 tablespoons of the milk and simmer until the cheese melts. If the mixture looks too thick, add more milk. Sprinkle the bread crumbs on top. (If you are not watching calories, you can add more grated cheese at this point.)

Bake in a 350-degree oven for 15 to 20 minutes.

Serves: 4 to 6
Heat Scale: Mild

〰〰〰〰〰〰

SPICY BAKED BEETS WITH GINGER AND CITRUS

This is a spicy vegetable side dish that can be served with many entrees and is guaranteed to bring raves. A yoga instructor once told us that beets are good for your liver, so this may even improve your health.

1   **pound fresh small beets**
1   **orange, peeled and sectioned**
2   **tablespoons orange juice concentrate**
1   **teaspoon fresh lime juice**
2   **teaspoons freshly grated ginger**

1   **tablespoon grated horseradish**
2   **tablespoons melted margarine**
1   **teaspoon New Mexican red chile powder**

Cut the tops off the fresh beets and scrub the beets thoroughly. Place the whole beets in a glass casserole dish and bake them at 350 degrees for 20 minutes. Using a sharp knife, pierce them to see if they are done. When they are done, remove them from the oven and let them cool enough to be peeled.

Peel the beets and slice them ¼ inch thick. Arrange in a baking dish with the orange sections.

Mix the remaining ingredients together and pour over the beets and oranges. Bake in a 350-degree oven for 10 to 15 minutes, or until the mixture is heated through.

Serves: 4
Heat Scale: Mild

〰〰〰〰〰〰〰〰

MULTI-NATIONAL SPICY EGGPLANT BAKE

We have been making this recipe for years, and it's a result of our travels to Greece, Israel, and Turkey where eggplant is served in a multitude of fashions. Sometimes the eggplants in your local grocery store are old and bitter, so look for smaller, unblemished ones; they are younger and sweeter. Or, better yet, grow your own and pick them when they are small; that's what we do. Or find out where your local farmers have a weekend market — that's where you can often find the freshest produce.

2	small eggplants	1	8-ounce can tomato sauce
¼	cup olive oil	1	ripe tomato, peeled, seeded, and diced
1	onion, chopped		
2	cloves garlic, chopped	¾	cup cooked rice (or ¾ cup cooked diced potatoes)
2	tablespoons chopped parsley		
3	tablespoons chopped fresh mint (or 1 tablespoon dried mint)	½	cup New Mexican green chiles, chopped fine (fresh or frozen)
2	teaspoons dried thyme		Parmesan cheese for garnish
1	teaspoon dried basil		

Wash the eggplants and slice in half horizontally. Using a sharp knife, cut around the inside of each eggplant, leaving about a ¼-inch "wall." Carefully scoop out the inside with a teaspoon. Reserve.

Heat the olive oil in a large skillet and sauté the eggplant, the onion, and the garlic for 3 minutes, taking care not to burn the garlic.

Then add the remaining ingredients and stir. Fill the eggplant halves with the mixture, mounding the tops. Arrange the halves in a baking dish. They should be close together so that they don't topple over.

Bake at 350 degrees for 40 minutes, or until the mixture is very hot and the sides of the eggplants are cooked. Sprinkle with grated Parmesan cheese if desired.

Serves: 2
Heat Scale: Mild

〰〰〰〰〰〰〰〰

SPICY SWEET POTATOES ANNA

Nothing is sacred in our constant creation of new and spicy recipes! We have taken the classic *pommes Anna* and given it a brand new twist in flavor. Dave always hated mushy, marshmallowy sweet potatoes, so we created this dish so he would eat his sweet potatoes and get his beta carotene. It was also a huge hit at our big Thanksgiving bash — even the kids were going back for seconds.

3 tablespoons melted margarine	3 tablespoons brown sugar
2 large sweet potatoes, peeled and sliced ¼ inch thick	½ teaspoon salt
1 tablespoon grated fresh ginger	¼ teaspoon freshly grated nutmeg
3 tablespoons frozen orange juice concentrate (or tangerine)	2 teaspoons New Mexican red chile powder

In a large bowl, combine all the ingredients and mix thoroughly to coat. In a 9-inch glass pie plate, arrange the coated slices in overlapping concentric circles; if it looks as if you will have a lot of coated sweet potatoes left over, put them in a second glass pie plate.

For fast cooking, microwave the potatoes for 3 to 4 minutes on high, then cover the plate with foil and weight it down with another pie plate filled with dried beans. Bake the potatoes for 20 minutes at 350 degrees. Remove the pie pan filled with beans and remove the foil from the sweet potatoes. Bake for another 20 to 35 minutes, or until the potatoes are slightly browned and crisp. (If you are not going to pre-cook with the microwave, allow 30 minutes for baking before you remove the foil; then bake again for 30 to 40 minutes.)

Serves: 4 to 6
Heat Scale: Mild

SAVORY SWISS CHARD PIE

If you are lucky enough to have a garden, you can pick your own onions, chard, and chile — and this main dish is literally yours. We like to serve it with Orange Gold Salad (see recipe, p. 71) and hot fresh bread, dripping with garlic and margarine. This combination makes a great light dinner or luncheon just short of spectacular with its great interplay of spices and seasonings.

½ cup minced onion

1 clove garlic, minced

¼ cup margarine

30 leaves Swiss chard, cleaned, dried, and torn into large pieces

2 eggs (or egg substitute), slightly beaten

⅓ cup chopped New Mexican green chile

½ cup grated cheese (use cheddar, Swiss, or Monterey Jack)

2 tablespoons bread crumbs

Preheat the oven to 350 degrees. Sauté the onion and garlic in the margarine until the onion is transparent, about 5 to 6 minutes. Add the chard and cook 1 minute or until chard wilts; be sure the chard is totally covered with the margarine. Spoon into a 9-inch pie pan.

Mix the eggs with the green chile and pour the mixture into the pie pan. Mix gently with a fork.

Sprinkle the cheese on top, then sprinkle on the bread crumbs.

Bake for 30 to 40 minutes, or until the pie is firm.

Serves: 5 to 6
Heat Scale: Mild

CLASSIC CILANTRO RATATOUILLE

Cilantro is the herb of choice for most traditional Mexican cuisines. We've added a little heat and eggplant to make this dish unforgettable.

1	medium eggplant, cut into 1-inch cubes	1	red bell pepper, coarsely chopped
1	tablespoon coarse salt	2	zucchinis, cut into 1-inch pieces
¼	cup olive oil		
2	stalks celery, cut into 1-inch pieces	6	tomatoes, quartered
2	medium leeks, cut into 1-inch pieces	1	cup Rich Vegetable Stock (see recipe, p. 5)
2	purple onions, cut into 1-inch pieces	1½	cups fresh cilantro, chopped
7	cloves garlic, chopped	3	tablespoons plus ⅓ cup sesame oil (not the Oriental concentrate variety)
4	new potatoes, quartered		
1	green bell pepper, coarsely chopped	1	tablespoon New Mexican red chile powder

Preheat the oven to 375 degrees. Place the eggplant in a colander. Toss with the salt and set aside for 1 hour to remove moisture. Pat dry with paper towels.

In a large skillet, heat the olive oil. Sauté the celery, leeks, onions, and garlic. Carefully remove the sautéed vegetables, leaving the oil in the skillet. Place the vegetables in a large ovenproof casserole dish.

Sauté the potatoes in the skillet for about 5 minutes, then add to the casserole. Next, increase the heat and stir-fry the red and green bell peppers and zucchinis in the skillet for about 5 minutes. Add this to the casserole with the tomatoes, broth, cilantro, 3 tablespoons of sesame oil, and the chile powder. Stir gently and bake for 30 minutes, uncovered.

Wipe out the skillet and add the ⅓ cup of sesame seed oil. Over medium heat, sauté the eggplant until tender. Stir the eggplant into the casserole and bake, covered, for 30 more minutes.

Serves: 8
Heat Scale: Mild

BALKAN AJVAR

This vegetable specialty was collected by Sharon Hudgins, contributing editor of *Chile Pepper,* who traveled extensively in the former Yugoslavia before the civil war began. She notes, "Pronounced *Eye-var,* this is a name of Turkish origin given to a popular type of dish made of roasted peppers and eggplant. Ripe red mild or medium-hot peppers are most often used, although green peppers, unripe tomatoes, and even string beans can be combined into *ajvar.* Fresh *ajvar* is always made during the late summer and early autumn, just after the pepper harvest — when many households also can or bottle their own *ajvar* for use throughout the year." Serve it as an appetizer to spread on thick slices of country-style white bread or flat pita bread, or use it as a side dish.

8 **to 12 fresh red New Mexican chiles (or substitute green chiles)**	1 **to 2 tablespoons lemon juice (or 1 tablespoon red wine vinegar)**
4 **medium-sized eggplants**	**Salt and pepper to taste**
½ **to ¾ cup olive oil (or corn oil)**	**Chopped fresh parsley, for garnish**
1 **large onion, minced**	
3 **large garlic cloves, finely chopped**	

Roast the chiles and eggplants over charcoal or a gas flame — or bake them in a preheated 475-degree oven — until the skins are blistered and black. Place the roasted vegetables in a paper bag and let them steam in their own heat for 10 minutes. Peel off and discard the burnt skins, along with the stems and seeds of the chiles. Mash the peppers and eggplant pulp together to form a homogenous mass — completely smooth or slightly chunky, as desired. You can do this in a food processor.

Heat 3 tablespoons of oil in a large skillet, and sauté the onion until very soft. Add the garlic and cook 2 minutes longer. Remove from the heat and stir in the pepper-eggplant pulp, mixing well. Slowly drizzle the remaining oil into the mixture, stirring constantly to incorporate all of the oil. Add lemon juice or vinegar, salt, and pepper, to taste. Transfer to a serving bowl and garnish with the parsley.

Yield: 6 to 8 servings, as an appetizer or side dish
Heat Scale: Medium

^^^^^^^^^^

EL RANCHO POTATOES

Here's one of our Sunday-brunch favorites, served after coming into the cool house after a hard couple of hours working in our chile garden. We usually make the potatoes to go with the Pancho Villa Omelette (see recipe, p. 159), but they could be paired with a number of other dishes in Chapter 6. If you like more heat, sprinkle the potatoes with your favorite hot sauce, or serve them with Ketchup with a Kick (see recipe, p. 8).

2   tablespoons olive oil
2   tablespoons margarine
2   cups cooked, cubed potatoes
½   cup diced onions
½   teaspoon ground cumin

2   teaspoons New Mexican red chile powder
½   green or red bell pepper, seeds removed, cut into ⅛-inch strips

Heat the olive oil and margarine in a large skillet and add the cubed potatoes, the onions, the cumin, and the red chile. Toss and turn the potatoes over medium heat until they start to brown. Then add the strips of bell pepper, and more olive oil if necessary. Keep tossing the potatoes with a spatula; make sure they brown evenly and don't burn. Serve hot.

Serves: 2
Heat Scale: Mild

YAPINGACHOS

Our friends who lived in Ecuador for two years told us this dish was freqently served there. It's a great one to know, because we always have that odd bit of cottage cheese hanging around — not enough to really do anything with, but on the other hand, we hate to throw it out. Since this recipe is starchy and cheesy, it can be served with grilled vegetables (which appear later on in this chapter) and a big green salad or a marinated bean salad. Ají chiles are used in Ecuador but are unavailable in the United States unless you grow them in your garden, as we do.

4	cups diced, peeled raw potatoes	½	cup small-curd, low-fat creamed cottage cheese
½	teaspoon salt	¼	cup chopped fresh chiles, such as yellow wax (or substitute jalapeños for more heat, or New Mexican green chiles for less)
1	egg yolk (or egg substitute)		
2	tablespoons cornstarch		
1½	cups chopped onion		
2	tablespoons margarine	¼	cup vegetable oil
½	cup freshly grated Parmesan cheese		

Place the potatoes in a large saucepan, cover with water, and add the salt. Bring to a boil and cook until tender, about 10 to 15 minutes. Drain and mash. Add the egg yolk and cornstarch and mix well.

Sauté the onions in the margarine until golden. Remove from the heat. Add the cheeses and the chile and mix well.

Shape the mashed-potato mixture into 10 balls, putting some of the cheese-chile mixture in the center of each.

Flatten the balls slightly and sauté in the hot oil until well browned on both sides.

Serves: 5 to 6
Heat Scale: Varies, but probably Medium

SPICY INDIAN CABBAGE AND COCONUT

If you want to be authentic, the shredded coconut should be from a fresh coconut and the green bell pepper should be curry leaf — a small pungent seasoning leaf that is sometimes available in specialty stores. Do not confuse the curry leaf with curry powders!

2	tablespoons vegetable oil	3½	ounces flaked coconut
½	teaspoon mustard seeds	1	medium cabbage, trimmed, quartered, cored, and sliced ½ inch thick
1	teaspoon crushed red piquin or santaka chiles		
1	large onion, chopped	½	teaspoon salt
2	tablespoons finely minced green bell pepper		

Heat the oil in a large, heavy Dutch oven over high heat; add the mustard seeds and stir until they pop (1 to 2 minutes). Lower the heat and add the crushed chiles, the onion, and the bell pepper. Stir-fry until the onion is golden, about 4 to 5 minutes. Mix in the coconut and stir-fry for 2 minutes.

Add the cabbage and the salt. Toss well until coated and glazed, about 5 minutes. Turn the heat to low, cover, and cook 12 to 15 minutes, until the cabbage is tender-crisp.

Serves: 6
Heat Scale: Medium

〜〜〜〜〜〜〜〜〜

PAPRIKA MUSHROOMS

Another great hot and spicy and meatless recipe from Sharon Hudgins, this one for *gombapaprikás* was collected in Hungary. Sharon described the procedure in *Chile Pepper* magazine: "To slice the mushrooms, use a hard-boiled-egg slicer. You'll be surprised how fast and easy it makes the preparation of this dish. In Hungary, this dish is served over toasted bread or rolls, or accompanied by dumplings or plain rice."

½ cup (1 stick) margarine

2 medium onions, chopped

1 pound fresh mushrooms (champignons, or a mixture of several kinds of mushrooms), cleaned and thinly sliced

1 large clove garlic, minced

1 rounded tablespoon mild paprika (or hot paprika, to taste)

½ teaspoon salt

1 cup low-fat sour cream

Melt the margarine in a large skillet over medium-high heat. Add the chopped onions and sauté until they are translucent. Add the sliced mushrooms and minced garlic. Stir until well combined and coated with the melted margarine. Reduce the heat to very low, sprinkle the paprika over the ingredients in the skillet, and mix well. Cover the skillet and simmer the mixture for about 10 minutes, or until the mushrooms begin to turn soft. Just before serving, add the salt and stir in the sour cream. Cook the mixture, stirring constantly, over low heat for 1 to 2 minutes, until the sour cream is warm. Do not let it boil. Serve immediately.

Serves: 4 to 6
Heat Scale: Mild

〜〜〜〜〜〜〜〜〜

GREEN BEANS À LA SIMON AND GARFUNKEL

Okay, we don't *really* know if it's their favorite dish, but with ingredients such as parsley, sage, rosemary, and thyme — and a little chile — we figured it would be a sure thing.

1½ cups green beans, trimmed

¼ cup margarine

1 teaspoon freshly chopped parsley (Italian preferred)

½ teaspoon sage

1½ teaspoons fresh rosemary, minced

½ teaspoon thyme

1 tablespoon ancho chile powder

⅓ cup freshly grated Parmesan cheese

Steam the green beans until they are *al dente*. In a large skillet, melt the margarine over moderate heat, adding the parsley, sage, rosemary, thyme, and chile powder. Add the beans, heating thoroughly, coating completely with the margarine-herb-chile combination. Remove the skillet from the heat and sprinkle the beans with Parmesan cheese.

Serves: 6
Heat Scale: Mild

∿∿∿∿∿∿∿∿∿∿∿

BRAISED BROCCOLI

Crisp-style cooking keeps this broccoli crunchy and green and appealing. Broccoli has always been a popular European vegetable, ever since the days of Catherine de' Medici, who even took it to France with her when she married. Broccoli has gotten a lot of bad press, but we think that's because most people overcook it.

¼ cup olive oil

1 shallot, minced

1 garlic clove, minced

1 teaspoon cayenne powder

2 pounds fresh broccoli florets

1 cup dry vermouth or dry white wine

Salt and pepper to taste

Heat the olive oil in a large skillet and sauté the shallots and the garlic for a few seconds. Then add the cayenne and the broccoli, and toss in the oil until coated. Add the remaining ingredients and bring the mixture to a boil. Reduce heat to low and simmer uncovered 3 to 5 minutes until crisp-tender. Transfer the broccoli to a heated dish.

Boil the remaining liquid until it is reduced to ½ cup and pour it over the broccoli.

Serves: 4 to 6
Heat Scale: Hot

~~~~~~~~~~~~~~~~

BLACKENED ITALIAN PEPPERS

Here's the first of our grilled vegetable recipes — a spicy starter that's easy and tastes great.

10 fresh Italian peppers (*pepperoncini*) (or substitute yellow wax hots)

12 ounces jalapeño cheese, cut into thick strips

Grill the Italian peppers over very hot coals, turning frequently to blacken evenly. After the peppers are fully charred, place in a covered bowl to cool. When they can be easily handled, cut the stem from each pepper, then make a slit in the side to remove the seeds. Place a thick strip of the jalapeño cheese in each pepper and return to the grill for an additional 3 minutes, or until the cheese is melted. Remove the skins and serve.

Serves: 5 as a side dish
Heat Scale: Mild to Medium

EARS AND BELLS OVER THE FIRE

Grilled corn is sheer heaven. Add a bell pepper or two, a spicy dressing and greens, and you've got a unique salad fit for any summer evening.

9	ears fresh corn in the husk	2¼	tablespoons sunflower oil
1	large red bell pepper	½	red onion, chopped
4½	tablespoons red cider vinegar		Fresh spinach leaves, torn into bite-size pieces
3	teaspoons honey		Salt and freshly ground pepper to taste
½	teaspoon cayenne powder		

Grill the ears of corn in their husks for 25 minutes over low heat, turning frequently. Place the bell pepper on the grill and continue to grill and turn until the husks are brown and the bell pepper is blackened.

Remove the vegetables from the heat and cool until each may be easily handled. Peel the bell pepper and chop into bite-size pieces. Remove the corn from the husks and cut the kernels from the cobs. Set aside.

In a large bowl, mix together the vinegar, honey, cayenne, and oil. Whisk vigorously. Add the corn, bell pepper, and onion. Toss with the fresh spinach leaves. Add salt and pepper to taste.

Serves: 6 as a side dish
Heat Scale: Medium

〰〰〰〰〰〰〰

GRILLED ORIENTAL VEGETABLES

Here's the essence of stir-fried vegetables without the hassle of an extra pan to wash. Feel free to vary the vegetables used.

1 cup snow peas
2 cups Chinese cabbage, chopped into ¼-inch pieces
1 can of straw mushrooms, drained
2 scallions, sliced in half
2 teaspoons sesame seed oil

2 teaspoons freshly grated ginger
2 teaspoons minced serrano or jalapeño chiles
½ teaspoon salt
1 teaspoon sesame seeds

In a bowl, combine the snow peas, cabbage, mushrooms, and scallions. Set aside. In another bowl, whisk together the oil, ginger, minced chiles, and salt. Coat the vegetables with the oil mixture. Place the vegetables on four 12-inch-square pieces of foil. Sprinkle sesame seeds onto the vegetables, then fold into packets, doubling the edges to seal. Grill on the edge of the rack, turning frequently to ensure that the vegetables are cooked evenly. Grill for about 10 minutes, or until the peas are *al dente*.

Serves: 4
Heat Scale: Medium

Fiery Foods: Fad or Trend? Part 5

"Chile peppers are the biggest food craze to hit the American palate since . . . well, since chocolate. True, garlic and barbecue have had their moments, and even their newsletters, but nothing like the spate of cookbooks, press hype, mail-order purveyors, posters, Christmas lights, and other collectibles that have followed in the wake of chilemania."
— John Thorne, *CookBook,* May–June, 1992

GRILLED SUMMER SQUASH
WITH LEMON GARLIC MARINADE

Here's a new way to prepare the tons of squash (especially zucchini) that all your gardening friends bring over.

3 **medium yellow squash, peeled and cut into quarters, lengthwise**	8 **cloves garlic**
	½ **cup lemon juice**
	½ **cup white wine**
3 **medium zucchinis, peeled and cut into quarters, lengthwise**	1 **teaspoon cayenne powder**

Place the squash in a deep bowl. In a food processor, puree the garlic, then add the lemon juice, white wine, and cayenne powder. Pour the garlic mixture over the squash and marinate for at least 3 hours. Cook the squash over a very hot grill, to mark the vegetables on each side. The squash is done when it is tender but still crisp. Remove from the heat and serve.

Serves: 8

Heat Scale: Medium to Hot

Note: Grill on a vegetable screen, so the squash doesn't fall onto the coals.

8

Tempting Breads and Cool-Down Desserts

I n this chapter we combine the breads and desserts, and the breads come first. The reason for this is, simply, that we eat far more breads than desserts. Now, don't get us wrong — we love desserts. But we also realize that because of their high levels of calories and fat, some desserts should be eaten only occasionally, or in such small amounts that it makes no sense to prepare them very often. So cooks should be forewarned that we have included some of these desserts, and those who object can omit them from their repertoire, or even simply eat fresh fruit for dessert.

Our collection of breads begins with spoonbreads, those pudding-like breads that are so soft that they are usually eaten with a spoon or fork. Three completely different spoonbreads are included — with varying chiles, other ingredients, and techniques — from Melissa, Mary Jane, and Dave. New Mexican Spoonbread, Melissa's recipe, uses New Mexican chiles; Ancho-Piquin Spoonbread, from Mary Jane, combines those two chiles, as expected; and Chipotle Spoonbread, Dave's favorite, uses smoke-dried jalapeños.

Breakfast breads are next, and we've got two great ones: Yogurt Scones with Red Chile Honey (try them at teatime) and the New Mexico favorite, Blue Corn Green Chile Muffins. Our selections for lunch and dinner include Carrot-Piñon Chile Bread (which Melissa calls addicting) and Smoke and Fire Skillet Bread, which features another smoked chile, the *morita*. Ethiopian Ambasha, an unusual spiced bread, is also included, as is Pumpkin Bread with No Chiles, our transition to desserts.

Our first dessert is our only spicy one: Black Pepper Strawberries, an unusual combination of flavors that's popular in Germany and France. Next, from Melissa, is her Low-Fat, Low-Guilt Chocolate Bars, which she swears will help people kick the Hershey habit. Classic Vanilla Flan is so common in New Mexico — probably the number one dessert served in the state — that we take it for granted and sometimes forget how great it tastes and how easy it is to prepare.

Citrus Pudding Cake is a spinoff on Key lime pie, with the richness on the bottom. Diet warning alarms sound with Mary Jane's Austrian Walnut Whipped Cream Torte, which comes straight from the old country via her grandmother. It is impossible to make this dessert using substitutes for sugar and eggs, so either splurge or skip it. The same warning applies to Melissa's The Wizard of Torte, which combines the flavors of tangerines and piñons. Just to prove that we can tone down the fattening ingredients, we offer Stoly Tea Cake — oops, there's vodka in it!

Pears Peloponnesian (or Poached Lady's Thighs), a Continental delicacy, are tasty, marinated, almond-filled pear halves. Another favorite fruit dessert of ours is Blackberry Lime Ice, a near–ice cream with a blackberry-citrus flavor.

Our final dessert is, appropriately enough, New Mexican Margarita Pie, which seems to contain every possible sinful ingredient from alcohol to sugar to whipped cream. We have included it because it is a great cool-down dessert with some of the flavors of our favorite place to live, the Southwest. Enjoy!

NEW MEXICAN SPOONBREAD

Our first entry in the spoonbread competition comes from Melissa, who prefers to use creamed corn *and* cornmeal. She sticks with New Mexican green chiles for the heat, combined with cheddar cheese.

1	16-ounce can cream-style corn (we prefer S & W brand for its high quality)	1	teaspoon baking powder
¾	cup low-fat milk	½	teaspoon salt (optional, or just add more green chile)
⅓	cup melted margarine	1	teaspoon sugar
1½	cups cornmeal	½	cup chopped New Mexican green chile
2	eggs, slightly beaten (or egg substitute)	1½	cups grated sharp cheddar cheese
½	teaspoon baking soda		

Mix all the ingredients together, except the chile and cheese. Pour half of the batter into a greased 9-by-9-inch pan, then sprinkle the batter with half of the green chile and half of the cheese. Add the remaining batter and top with the other half of the chile and cheese. Bake at 400 degrees for 45 minutes.

Serves: 6
Heat Scale: Mild

〰〰〰〰〰〰

ANCHO-PIQUIN SPOONBREAD

Our second entry in the heavier spoonbread competition comes from Mary Jane, who has opted for a combination of anchos (for their raisiny flavor) and piquins (for their heat). This spicy spoonbread is an ideal side dish for grilled vegetables (see Chapter 7), with or without a spicy grill sauce.

2 **tablespoons vegetable oil**	2 **teaspoons ancho chile powder**
1/4 **cup diced green bell peppers**	1/2 **teaspoon piquin chile powder**
1 **small onion, minced**	1/2 **teaspoon baking soda**
2 **pounds tomatoes, peeled and diced but not drained (or substitute 1 28-ounce can of tomatoes)**	1/2 **teaspoon salt**
1 **cup cornmeal**	1 **cup shredded Monterey Jack cheese**
1 **egg (or egg substitute)**	**Milk as needed**

Heat the oil and sauté the bell peppers and the onion for 2 minutes. Add the tomatoes to the mixture and set aside in a bowl for 10 minutes. Then stir in the cornmeal, egg, chile powders, baking soda, salt, and cheese and mix thoroughly. If the mixture seems extremely thick, add milk (by the tablespoon) until it is thick but pourable. Pour into a well-greased 1½-quart casserole. Bake in a 350-degree oven for 1 hour or until firm. Serve hot.

Serves: 4 to 6
Heat Scale: Medium

∿∿∿∿∿∿∿∿∿∿∿∿

CHIPOTLE SPOONBREAD

Dave's spoonbread features chipotle chiles, those smoky-hot jalapeños that come canned in adobo sauce. The heat level can aways be adjusted downward if desired. Dried chipotles can be used if they are soaked in water for 30 minutes before pureeing.

2½ cups low-fat milk
1   cup yellow cornmeal
3   eggs (or egg substitute)
2   teaspoons sugar
½   teaspoon salt
4   tablespoons melted margarine

1   teaspoon thyme or marjoram
1   teaspoon baking powder
3   chipotle chiles, pureed without the adobo sauce
½   cup grated jalapeño

Heat 2 cups of the milk to simmering and stir in the cornmeal. When the mixture is thick, remove it from the heat.

Beat the eggs well, then mix in the remaining ½ cup of milk, the sugar, the salt, and the melted margarine. Combine with the hot cornmeal mixture. Stir in the thyme or marjoram, baking powder, and pureed chipotles. Mix thoroughly. Pour into a well-greased 1½-quart baking dish or casserole. Bake in a 400-degree oven for 45 minutes or until the spoonbread is firm and lightly browned. Spoon onto plates and serve at once.

Serves: 6
Heat Scale: Hot

But We Love This Aroma in New Mexico

The main street of Tiburon, California, was evacuated on August 8, 1992, because of an "acrid stink" or "funny smell" that officials thought might be a toxic leak. You guessed it — the Guaymas Restaurant was roasting chiles.

YOGURT SCONES WITH RED CHILE HONEY

Here is a perfect breakfast or tea time treat; cut the calories and add some heat! Red chile honey has become quite popular in New Mexico and other parts of the Southwest.

2⅔ cups unbleached all-purpose flour	1 egg, separated
3 teaspoons sugar	1 cup low-fat plain yogurt
1 teaspoon baking powder	1 tablespoon water
6 tablespoons chilled margarine, cut into small pieces	1 cup pure honey
1 egg (or egg substitute)	1 tablespoon New Mexican red chile powder (or hotter powder, to taste)

Preheat the oven to 400 degrees. Combine the flour, sugar, and baking powder in a large bowl. Using a pastry blender or two knives, cut the margarine into the mixture until it resembles coarse meal. Mix the whole egg and the yolk of the separated egg together and stir into the batter. Blend in the yogurt. Set the leftover egg white aside in a bowl.

Turn the mixture out onto a lightly floured surface. Knead briefly until the dough sticks together. Roll out to a thickness of 1 inch. Cut with a 2-inch biscuit cutter (a coyote-shaped cutter works well). Gather together the leftover dough; reroll and cut additional scones. Place all the cut dough on a greased cookie sheet.

Mix the egg white and water. Brush the top of each scone with this glaze. Bake about 14 minutes, or until golden brown.

Meanwhile, mix the red chile powder into the honey until all the chile is evenly distributed. Serve immediately with the freshly baked scones.

Yield: 12 scones
Heat Scale: Mild, although the red chile honey
will definitely add a little zip!

BLUE CORN GREEN CHILE MUFFINS

Blue corn, or Indian corn, has become increasingly popular, and there are now blue corn tortillas, corn meal, and chips. It has a nuttier flavor than regular corn and gives these muffins a delightful — some say shocking — color.

1½ cups fine-ground blue corn meal (available by mail order and from gourmet shops)	¼ cup onions, minced
	1 clove garlic, minced
1 cup all-purpose flour	2 large eggs (or egg substitute)
1 tablespoon salt	1 cup low-fat milk
1 tablespoon baking powder	½ cup chopped New Mexican green chile
2 tablespoons sugar	2 tablespoons fresh cilantro, chopped
1¾ sticks margarine, melted	

Preheat the oven to 450 degrees. Combine the blue corn meal, flour, salt, baking powder, and sugar in a large bowl. In another bowl, whisk together the margarine, onion, and garlic. Add the eggs, milk, chile, and cilantro, whisking continually.

Add the flour mixture in small amounts until the batter is completely combined. Pour the batter into 12 well-greased ½-cup muffin tins. Bake the muffins for 18 to 20 minutes, or until they are golden. Turn them out onto racks and let them cool.

Yield: 12 muffins
Heat Scale: Medium

CARROT-PIÑON CHILE BREAD

With carrots, chile, and piñons as its principal ingredients, this bread is positively addicting. It's a spicy-sweet concoction sure to leave one day-dreaming of warm sultry days in the islands — or on the mesa.

1½ cups all-purpose flour, sifted	½ cup vegetable oil
1½ teaspoons baking soda	1 teaspoon vanilla
¼ teaspoon cinnamon	½ teaspoon salt
1 tablespoon New Mexican red chile powder	1½ cups grated carrots
¾ cup sugar	1½ cups ground piñons or pine nuts
2 eggs, beaten (or egg substitute)	

Preheat the oven to 350 degrees. In a large mixing bowl, sift together the flour, baking soda, cinnamon, and chile powder. In another bowl, mix the sugar, eggs, oil, vanilla, and salt. Add the sifted ingredients to the egg mixture, stirring until the batter is smooth and the ingredients are well distributed. Fold in the carrots and piñons. Pour into a greased 9-by-5-inch loaf pan. Bake about 1 hour.

Remove the bread pan from the oven and place it on a rack for about 10 minutes. Remove the bread from the pan and place on the rack to cool completely.

Yield: 1 loaf
Heat Scale: Medium

〰〰〰〰〰〰〰

SMOKE AND FIRE SKILLET BREAD

Smoked serranos, also known as *moritas,* are the main ingredient of this easy-to-make bread. They are available by mail order or in Latin markets. Chipotles may be substituted for them. Tell your friends it took you hours to conjure up the rich and distinctive smoky flavors within — we won't tell!

Vegetable oil	**1¼ cups all-purpose flour**
1 cup low-fat milk	**1 cup yellow cornmeal**
6 tablespoons margarine, melted	**2 tablespoons sugar**
2 smoked serrano chiles (or substitute 2 chipotles in adobo sauce)	**1½ teaspoons baking powder**
	1 teaspoon salt
1 egg	**1 cup grated Monterey Jack cheese**

Preheat the oven to 450 degrees. Using enough vegetable oil to cover, grease a 10-inch-wide cast-iron skillet with 2-inch-high sides. Heat the skillet in the oven for 18 minutes.

While the skillet is heating up, combine the milk, margarine, serranos, and egg in a food processor and blend until the chiles are finely chopped. In a large bowl, combine the flour, cornmeal, sugar, baking powder, and salt. Add the processed milk mixture and the grated cheese to the dry ingredients and stir until well combined.

Pour the batter into the preheated skillet. Bake 15 to 20 minutes, or until a toothpick inserted into the center comes out clean. Cool for a few minutes before cutting into wedges.

Serves: 8
Heat Scale: Medium

‸‸‸‸‸‸‸‸‸‸‸‸‸‸

ETHIOPIAN AMBASHA

Our thanks to *Chile Pepper* contributor Nanette Blanchard for this exotic bread, which is baked in a pizza pan and is topped with *berbere* seasonings (spices from a North African hot sauce). Nanette says that the spices can also be incorporated into the dough itself. Because this recipe makes a stickier dough than usual breads, we do not recommend using a food processor.

1 tablespoon active dry yeast	1 teaspoon ground fenugreek
¼ cup warm water (110 degrees)	2 teaspoons salt
2 tablespoons ground coriander	⅓ cup vegetable oil
1 teaspoon ground cardamom	1¼ cups lukewarm water
½ teaspoon ground white pepper	5 cups unbleached flour

TOPPING

1 tablespoon ground hot red chile, such as cayenne or piquin	¼ teaspoon ground ginger
	Pinch of ground cloves
2 tablespoons vegetable oil	⅛ teaspoon cinnamon

Dissolve the yeast in the ¼ cup of warm water and let stand for 10 minutes. Then, to the yeast mixture, add the coriander, cardamom, white pepper, fenugreek, salt, oil, and the 1¼ cups of water, and stir well. Slowly add the flour until a mass forms. On a floured board, knead the dough for 10 minutes or until it is smooth and tiny bubbles form.

Reserve a piece of dough about 1 inch in diameter. With floured hands, spread the rest of the dough out on an ungreased pizza pan in the shape of a circle. Using a sharp knife, score the dough in a design similar to the spokes of a bicycle wheel. Place the reserved ball of dough in the center of the scored dough. Cover and let rise for one hour.

Bake at 350 degrees for an hour or until golden brown.

Combine the topping ingredients in a small bowl. While the bread is still warm, brush the top with the topping.

Yield: 1 16-inch round, flat bread

Heat Scale: Medium

PUMPKIN BREAD WITH NO CHILES

This is a recipe that Mary Jane has been making for years — it's a variation on a recipe her mother gave her. It is a fairly sweet, heavy bread that was originally served as a dessert, but it can also be served with a big summer salad or with a hearty soup in the winter. This bread can be served hot or at room temperature, and it also freezes very well.

1 **cup brown sugar, firmly packed**

½ **cup granulated sugar**

1 **cup cooked or canned pumpkin**

½ **cup vegetable oil (or substitute ¼ cup oil and ¼ cup unsweetened apple sauce)**

2 **eggs, unbeaten (or egg substitute)**

2 **cups sifted all-purpose flour**

1 **teaspoon baking soda**

¼ **teaspoon salt**

½ **teaspoon nutmeg (freshly ground preferred)**

½ **teaspoon cinnamon**

¼ **teaspoon ground ginger**

1 **cup raisins (optional)**

½ **cup chopped walnuts or pecans**

¼ **cup water**

Preheat the oven to 350 degrees.

Combine the sugar, pumpkin, oil (or oil and apple sauce), and eggs. Beat until well blended. In another bowl, sift together the flour, soda, salt, and spices and add to the pumpkin-sugar; mix well. Stir in the raisins, nuts, and water. Pour the mixture into a well-greased 9-by-5-by-3-inch loaf pan. Bake at 350 degrees for 65 to 75 minutes, or until well done (when a toothpick inserted into it comes out clean). Remove from the baking pan and cool on a wire rack.

Yield: 1 large loaf

BLACK PEPPER STRAWBERRIES

This recipe is as close as we're going to get to a hot and spicy dessert. During strawberry season in Europe, this dessert can be found in many restaurants. It is an unusual combination of ingredients, and if you're feeling decadent and are throwing calories to the wind, top the berries with a dollop of sweetened whipped cream.

2	pints strawberries, washed and hulled	3	tablespoons granulated sugar
3	teaspoons fresh lemon juice	1½	teaspoons freshly ground black pepper
4	tablespoons fresh orange juice		

Place the drained berries in a large bowl and sprinkle the top with the remaining ingredients. Toss gently to coat; marinate the berries for 1 hour in the refrigerator. Spoon into stemmed glasses and serve.

Serves: 6 to 8

^^^^^^^^^^^^^^^^^^^

LOW-FAT, LOW-GUILT CHOCOLATE BARS

Make this chocolate goodie for yourself and a guest, and make no apologies. We've cut out most of the mental and physical anguish associated with this rich treat. We've slashed the fat, so any guilt remaining at all resides in the sugar — which would be difficult to eliminate from this recipe.

3	ounces unsweetened chocolate, chopped	3	egg whites
1	cup granulated sugar	1	teaspoon vanilla extract
¾	cup flour	¼	teaspoon salt
¾	cup 2 percent low-fat cottage cheese, at room temperature		Powdered sugar

Preheat the oven to 350 degrees.

In a saucepan over very low heat, or in a double boiler, melt the chocolate. Remove from the heat and cool slightly. Combine the granulated sugar, flour, cottage cheese, egg whites, vanilla, and salt in a food processor and puree until smooth. Add the melted chocolate and blend well. Pour the batter into a lightly greased 8-inch-square pan.

Bake for 20 to 25 minutes, or until just set. Remove from the oven and sprinkle with powdered sugar. Cool and cut into bars.

Yield: 16 bars

Nasal Warfare

Researchers at Johns Hopkins University are testing a nasal spray loaded with capsaicin in an attempt to relieve the suffering of people with chronic sneezing and runny noses. The testing, performed on volunteers, first caused them to sneeze their heads off and their noses to drip, drip, drip.

But after a while, the volunteers stopped sneezing and their noses stopped running — thanks to the flushing effect of the capsaicin. There seems to be no end in sight to the medical applications of capsaicin.

CLASSIC VANILLA FLAN

This flan always makes an elegant dessert; a bonus is that it is easy to make and the recipe is foolproof. The recipe comes from Mary Jane's former landlady in Cuernavaca, Mexico, who loved good food, but didn't like to spend long hours in the kitchen.

3 tablespoons brown sugar, mixed with 1 tablespoon of water	Enough milk to fill the empty can from the condensed milk
1 can sweetened condensed milk (Eagle brand is the one we prefer)	3 eggs 1 teaspoon vanilla extract

In a small, heavy saucepan, melt the sugar mixed with the water and caramelize it by heating it until it is thick and brown. Coat a 1½-quart Pyrex casserole with the sugar mixture.

Pour the condensed milk into a blender. Fill the empty can with milk and pour that into the blender, along with the eggs and vanilla. Blend at high speed for one minute. Carefully pour this mixture into the coated Pyrex casserole.

Place the casserole in a water bath. The water should come about 2 inches up the outer sides of the casserole. Bake, uncovered, in a 350-degree oven for 50 to 60 minutes. The middle of the flan, like custard, should still be a little "jiggly," so do not overbake. Remove the flan from the oven and allow it to reach room temperature before it is refrigerated. The flan can be served slightly warm or chilled. Spoon the custard into small dessert bowls and spoon some of the brown-sugar mixture over the flan.

Serves: 6

CITRUS PUDDING CAKE

Here's a twist on Key lime pie, which is also one of our favorites. As the mixture bakes, the cake forms a light sponge layer with a rich, delicious sauce below it. It can be served warm or chilled.

3	tablespoons margarine	¼	Key lime juice (or substitute regular lime or lemon juice)
1	cup sugar		
¼	cup flour		
3	eggs, separated	1½	cups low-fat milk
2	teaspoons lime zest	¼	teaspoon salt

Preheat the oven to 325 degrees.

Cream the margarine, ½ cup of the sugar, and the flour together. Add the egg yolks and beat well. Stir in the lime zest, lime juice, and milk. Set this mixture aside.

Add the salt to the egg whites and beat until stiff. Gradually beat in the remaining ½ cup of sugar. Fold this mixture into the first mixture.

Pour the batter into a 1½-quart greased baking dish and set the dish in a large, shallow pan containing boiling water 1 inch deep. Bake in a 325-degree oven for 1 hour.

Serves: 6

∿∿∿∿∿∿∿∿

AUSTRIAN WALNUT WHIPPED CREAM TORTE

This torte is one of Mary Jane's favorite desserts, and it comes from the vast files of her grandmother Wilan, the woman who would whip up an enormous apple strudel on a moment's notice. Although this dessert looks rich, it is surprisingly light and refreshing, probably because of the bread crumbs; however, it is not light on the calories and fat. Make it for special occasions; we all have to splurge sometimes!

6   eggs, separated
¾   cup sugar
¾   cup bread crumbs
¾   cup finely ground
     walnuts

1   teaspoon vanilla
     flavoring
1   pint whipping cream
     Ground walnuts for
     garnish (optional)

Beat the egg yolks with the sugar for 15 minutes, until the mixture is light and frothy. In a separate bowl, beat the egg whites until they are stiff.

Alternately add the egg whites and bread crumbs into the yolk mixture. Then fold in the ground nuts and the vanilla.

Pour the mixture into two 8-inch ungreased cake pans, dividing it evenly between the two pans. Bake at 350 degrees for 30 minutes.

Remove the cake from the oven and allow it to cool before removing it from the pans. When the cake is cool, run a sharp knife around the edges of the pans and use a spatula to loosen the bottoms of the cake. Invert it back onto the cooling racks.

Cut each layer in half horizontally with a serrated knife. Place one of the halves onto a cake plate and spread with about ½ inch of the whipped cream. Place another half on top of the first one and spread with the whipped cream; repeat with the other 2 halves. When all the layers are filled, frost the sides of the cake with the whipped cream and smooth the top. Additional ground nuts can be sprinkled over the top and sides of the cake if desired.

Serves: 8

〜〜〜〜〜〜〜〜〜

THE WIZARD OF TORTE

Chocolate, piñons, and tangerines — oh, my! Melissa comments, "Until this recipe, I never seemed to have the courage, heart, or brain to make a torte come out well. Finally, a dessert that makes friends say there's no place like my home!"

1½ cups piñons or pine nuts
1 tablespoon tangerine peel, coarsely chopped
¾ cup all-purpose flour
½ cup unsweetened cocoa powder
1 teaspoon baking powder
Dash of salt
2 large eggs, not chilled
2 large egg whites, not chilled

1 cup granulated sugar
¾ cup vegetable oil
¼ cup tangerine juice, freshly squeezed (or substitute frozen orange juice)
1 teaspoon vanilla extract
Powdered sugar

Preheat the oven to 350 degrees. Lightly grease a 10-inch cake pan. Coat it lightly with flour, shaking off the excess. Chop the piñons and tangerine peel finely in a food processor. In a large bowl, combine the flour, cocoa powder, baking powder, and salt. Add the piñon mixture to the flour mixture and stir well.

With an electric mixer, beat the eggs and egg whites in a large bowl until frothy. Slowly add the granulated sugar, beating until the mixture is light yellow in color, about 5 minutes.

Put the mixer on low speed and add the vegetable oil. While still beating on slow speed, add the tangerine juice and vanilla. Gently fold this mixture into the flour/piñon mixture until completely blended.

Pour batter into the greased and floured cake pan. Bake the torte about 35 minutes, or until the edges of the cake begin to pull away from the side of the pan and the center is firm to the touch.

Remove the cake from the oven; place on a rack to cool. Remove the cake from the pan, place on a platter, and sprinkle the top of the cake with powdered sugar.

Yield: 8 large or 16 small servings

STOLY TEA CAKE

With this basic tea cake recipe, you can create your own signature cake — that's the one everyone asks you to make for the next potluck or buffet party. It's also fun to experiment. The Stolichnaya–blueberry–lemon zest mix is a good one, but so is a semi-spicy one combining Absolut Peppar vodka, lemon zest, and ground red chile.

1 cup margarine, at room temperature	1/2 cup low-fat milk
1 teaspoon grated lemon rind	1 1/2 cups blueberries, preferably fresh (if using frozen, drain well and dry on paper towels)
1 1/3 cups of sugar	
2 eggs (or egg substitute)	Juice of 1 large lemon
1 1/2 cups flour	Rind of 1/2 lemon, grated
1/2 teaspoon salt	1/2 cup vodka (Stolichnaya preferred)
1 teaspoon baking powder	

Preheat the oven to 350 degrees and grease a standard-size glass loaf pan (9-by-5-inch).

Cream the margarine, the 1 teaspoon of grated lemon rind, and 1 cup of the sugar together until light and fluffy. Add the eggs, one at a time, beating thoroughly after each addition.

Sift the flour with the salt and baking powder. Add this mixture alternately with the milk, beating well after each addition. Add the blueberries and gently fold into the batter. Pour the batter into the greased loaf pan and bake for 45 minutes at 350 degrees.

While the tea cake is baking, mix the remaining 1/3 cup of sugar in a saucepan with the lemon juice and grated rind of 1/2 lemon, and heat until the sugar is dissolved; add the vodka and stir. Set aside. When the cake has finished baking, pour the lemon-vodka mixture over the top of the cake while the cake is still hot. Allow it to cool before removing it from the pan.

Serves: 8 to 10

PEARS PELOPONNESIAN, OR POACHED LADY'S THIGHS

When pears are in season, this dessert is a refreshing one to serve, even though the ancient Sumerians thought of the pear more as a medicine than as a dessert! The ever-sensual medieval French, undoubtedly searching for another aphrodisiac, called the fruit *cuisse-dame,* or "lady's thigh."

THE PEARS AND SYRUP

6	pears, peeled and carefully cored	½	teaspoon ground cinnamon
2	cups dry red wine	½	cup sugar
2	tablespoons fresh lemon juice	2	cups cold water

Add the pears to the remaining ingredients in a saucepan and bring to a boil; reduce the heat to medium-high and poach the pears for 8 to 10 minutes, stirring once or twice. Remove the pan from the heat and allow the pears to cool in the syrup for about 20 minutes. Then drain them on a rack.

THE FILLING

1	egg, or egg substitute	3	tablespoons margarine
1	egg yolk	2	teaspoons vanilla flavoring
¾	cup sugar		
½	cup flour, sifted	¼	teaspoon almond extract
1	cup hot low-fat milk	½	cup ground almonds

To make the filling, beat together the egg and the yolk, gradually adding the sugar and then the flour. Continue beating and add the hot milk slowly until the mixture is thoroughly combined. Heat the mixture in a heavy saucepan over moderate heat and stir slowly with a whisk. When the mixture begins to lump, beat it quickly until it smoothes and thickens into a paste. Lower the heat and stir with a spoon for 2 minutes, then remove the mixture from the heat and beat in the remaining ingredients.

THE SAUCE

2 cups fresh or frozen raspberries	¼ cup sugar, or more to taste

To make the sauce, blend the raspberries and sugar together in a blender and strain the mixture through a sieve to remove the seeds.

To prepare and serve the dessert, fill the cores of the pears with the almond filling and spoon the sauce lightly over the pears.

Serves: 6

BLACKBERRY LIME ICE

This near–ice cream is designed to cool down the most inflamed mouth while giving a fruity finish to the palate. Any berries in season can be used. Serve it in hollowed lemon halves with a sprig of fresh mint as a garnish.

3 cups blackberries	2 teaspoons unflavored gelatin
¼ cup strained fresh lime juice	1½ cups sugar
1½ teaspoons grated lime rind	3 cups water

Puree the blackberries, lime juice, and lime rind in a food processor equipped with a steel blade. A blender will also work, but make sure to puree in batches. Strain the pureed mixture through a fine sieve into a bowl, pressing hard on any solid pieces of blackberry or lemon.

Sprinkle the gelatin over the puree; let it soften for 15 minutes.

Combine the sugar and water in a stainless steel saucepan. Stir until the sugar is dissolved, bringing the mixture to a boil over moderate heat. Reduce the heat and simmer for 5 minutes. Remove the pan from the heat, add the blackberry mixture, and stir until the gelatin is dissolved. Let the mixture cool, then chill in the refrigerator, covered, for 1 hour or until it is cold to the touch.

Divide the mixture evenly between two ice cube trays without the dividers. Place in the freezer for 3 to 4 hours, or until it is firm but not frozen hard.

When the mixture is sufficiently frozen, transfer it to a food processor (steel blade still intact) and beat until the mixture is smooth but still partially frozen. Return to the ice trays and freeze for 1 to 2 hours, or until frozen.

Serves: 10 or more

〰〰〰〰〰〰〰〰〰〰

NEW MEXICAN MARGARITA PIE

This recipe will leave you with neither a hangover nor leftovers! It is a perfect finish to any of the hot and spicy combinations in this cookbook.

THE CRUST

6 tablespoons margarine	2 tablespoons granulated sugar
1½ cups finely ground unsalted pretzels	

Place the margarine in a 9-inch glass pie plate and microwave it on high for 1 to 2 minutes, or until the margarine is melted.

Stir in the pretzel crumbs and granulated sugar. Press the mixture against the sides and bottom of the dish to form an even crust. Microwave on high for 1 to 2 minutes, or until the crust sets.

THE FILLING

1 cup granulated sugar	1 tablespoon Triple Sec
3 tablespoons cornstarch	1 cup low-fat yogurt
¼ cup margarine	1 cup whipping cream
2 teaspoons grated lime rind	2 tablespoons confectioner's sugar
½ cup freshly squeezed lime juice	2 whole limes, very thinly sliced, for garnish
½ cup half-and-half	Coarse salt
¼ cup tequila	

Combine the granulated sugar, cornstarch, margarine, grated lime rind, lime juice, and half-and-half in a 2-quart microwave-safe casserole dish. Microwave on high for 2 minutes. Stir well. Microwave on high again for 1 to 3 minutes, or until thickened.

With an electric mixer, beat the mixture until smooth, 1 to 2 minutes. Beat in the tequila and Triple Sec. Refrigerate the mixture for about 1 hour, or speed-cool in the freezer for 20 minutes. When the mixture is cool, fold in the yogurt.

Pour the filling into the prepared pie shell. Smooth the top evenly with a knife.

Whip the cream and sweeten it with the confectioner's sugar. Spoon the whipped cream on top of the pie.

Dip half of each lime slice into the coarse salt. Place the unsalted sides of the lime slices around the rim of the pie. Chill for at least 1 hour before serving.

Serves: 8

Firewater

Miss Manners is completely baffled. Emily Post has no clue whatsoever. In fact, there's a crisis these days in the world of etiquette because none of the experts can answer this question: What drinks should be served with hot and spicy foods?

The turmoil has been caused by the fact that more and more Americans are consuming hot and spicy dishes from a number of world cuisines, yet most cookbook authors and magazine writers on the subject have avoided matching beverages to the sizzling entrees. Should peppery cocktails, such as those made with chile pepper vodkas, be served with spicy foods, or is such a practice culinary overkill? Which wines should be matched with the enormous variety of exotic, incendiary dishes? What role does beer play in this question? And isn't it only polite to provide cool-down drinks for guests whose palates have not yet adapted to the heat levels of the fiery food being served?

We are pleased to announce that we have answered these questions and resolved once and for all the problem of fiery-food beverage etiquette. The task was not an easy one. It required long hours of research, testing, and repeated tasting of alcoholic and nonalcoholic beverages in combination with chile-peppered victuals, but somehow we succeeded. The key was the realization that in a typically lavish fiery feast, the beverages are served in a very consistent pattern: before, during, and after the main courses. Therefore, firewater — the generic term for these drinks — should follow this pattern.

PEPPERY COCKTAILS

Since cocktails always precede the meal, it makes perfect sense that a burning beverage is the best way to prepare guests for the fiery feast to follow. The most basic peppery cocktail is one that has the heat already in it — namely, a liquor that has been treated with some variety of chile pepper.

It is ironic that chile pepper–flavored liquors originated in a country virtually devoid of fiery foods: the Soviet Union. The word *vodka* is the Russian diminutive for *water,* which gives us a fairly good indication of just how basic and important this liquor is in the Soviet Union. In fact, the people there love it so much they cannot leave it alone. They blend about forty different flavors of various herbs and spices with their vodkas, including combinations of heather, mint, nutmeg, cloves, cinnamon — and, of course, cayenne powder.

A favorite brand of Russian chile-pepper vodka is *Stolichnaya Pertsovka,* the famous "Stoly," which has been infused with white and black pepper combined with cayenne powder, and then filtered to remove all solids. Unfortunately, the reddish tint of the vodka is the result of added caramel coloring rather than the color of the chiles, but it still tastes great and has a nice bite. Other popular brands of hot vodka are Absolut Peppar from Sweden and America's own Gordon's Pepper-Flavored Vodka.

Today, Bloody Marys are often made with the chile-infused vodkas, and variations on the Bloody Mary include replacing the vodka with tequila — which creates a "Bloody Maria" — or with Japanese *sake* for a "Bloody Mary Quite Contrary." The cocktail can be made with one of the chile-pepper vodkas to supply the pungency, or it can be spiced up with a favorite brand of bottled hot sauce. Since each of the various chiles used in these sauces has its own unique flavor, the taste of the Bloody Marys can vary significantly. Tabasco Sauce, the trademarked brand of McIlhenny Company, is still the hot sauce most commonly used to spice up this drink, but these days people are experimenting with hot sauces based on the cayenne, habanero, jalapeño, and even chipotle chiles.

It is always embarrassing to discover — after you've served the peppery cocktails — that one of your guests has recently been discharged from an alcohol treatment center. So for guests on the wagon, serve them a volatile Virgin Mary, which retains the hot sauce but eliminates the vodka.

Our cocktails for this book include three highly spiced creations and other, "normal" cocktails that go well with hot and spicy foods. The spicy cocktails are: Tex-Mex Liquors, in which we infuse tequila or vodka with fiery chiltepins; A Purist's Perfectly Pungent Bloody Mary, which we immodestly claim is the world's best; and Hot Tequila, Frozen Margarita, a contradiction in terms but not in taste. The "normal" cocktails are Tropical Rum Slush, a perfect island cooler, and Chimayo Cocktail, which combines cider and tequila.

MATCHING WINES AND BEERS WITH SPICY ENTREES

The fiery main courses have been selected, whether at home or in a restaurant. But what beverages should accompany such incendiary dishes as the ones contained in the other chapters of this book? Certainly not the same peppery cocktail you've been drinking before the meal, because the pungency of the drink will mask the complex flavors and spiciness of the entree. Since wines and beers are traditionally served with meals all over the world, the crucial questions to answer are: Will the fiery foods overwhelm the wine, and do wines and beers extinguish the fire of the chiles?

Wine expert Roy Andries de Groot believes that wines do indeed cut the heat of chile dishes. He suggests serving cold white wines with most spicy foods and claims that a Chablis, Chenin Blanc, or Colombard is "excellent for putting out chile fires." Undoubtedly he has heard the argument that beer and wine have some efficacy as cool-downs because capsaicin — the chemical that gives chiles their heat — dissolves readily in alcohol but does not mix with water. This theory holds that the alcohol dilutes the capsaicin and thus reduces the heat sensation. However, since both beer and wine are more than 80 percent water, the alcohol content actually has little effect on the heat levels.

So do not expect wines and beers to reduce the pungency of the dishes being served. Although the cool temperature at which many beers and wines are served may give the illusion of reducing heat, in reality they do not temper the sting of capsaicin very much and in some cases may even increase it. Beverage consultant Ronn Wiegand, writing in Marlena Spieler's book *Hot & Spicy,* warns, "The tannin content of most young red wines can actually magnify the heat."

With beer and wine accompaniments, the heat level is not nearly as important as a harmonious blending of flavors and textures. For example, we usually drink beer with the hottest Mexican and Chinese foods because it is a perfect complement, not because of its reputation as a cool-down. With some of the spicy New Southwest meals, slightly fruity white wines such as Chenin Blancs or Rieslings seem to be a better pairing.

Roy Andries de Groot has studied the problem of which wines to serve with fiery foods and advises, "My theory of the successful marriage of wine with these cuisines is to know (and separate) the gentle dishes, the spicy dishes, and the fiery dishes. The menu is then planned so that each group of dishes is paired with the wine that adds certain essential contrasts and harmonies."

For example, he recommends a Bordeaux or a Cabernet Sauvignon as the best wine to accompany the chocolate-flavored *mole poblano* and calls the combination "one of the more memorable marriages of exotic gastronomy." For curries, de Groot suggests a Fumé Blanc or a soft Semillon; for the entrees that top the heat scale he has surprising advice — an American light wine. Since he believes that white wine cuts the heat, he advises that the wine should be low in alcohol so it can be consumed in great quantities without discomfort.

Ronn Wiegand recommends serving the wine that your budget can comfortably accommodate. He suggests that fine and rare wines are not perfect beverages with fiery foods because their "flavor nuances" are overwhelmed by the strong spices, but admits that there are times when no other drink will do. "At such times," he writes, "simply upgrade the quality of the wine you would normally serve with a given dish, and enjoy the inevitable fireworks."

When deciding which beers to offer guests who are about to assault their senses with chile heat, one logical solution is to do a regional match: Carta Blanca with Mexican foods, a Tsingtao with Sichuan dishes, Tusker with African entrees, Red Stripe with Jamaican foods, and so on. With American spicy specialties, such as New Mexican or

Cajun, we suggest forgetting every American beer that is advertised on TV — they are all mediocre at best. Instead, serve one of the finer regional specialty beers such as Capitol or Augsburger from Wisconsin, or Anchor Steam from San Francisco.

Incidentally, some writers insist that dark beers should never be served with spicy foods because they are traditionally served in cool climates rather than tropical ones. Such a judgment makes little culinary sense because often one needs a heavy, dark beer to match a meal measuring 8 or more on the heat scale. Besides, the theory is proven false in Mexico, where such fine dark beers as Negra Modelo and Dos Equis are commonly served with the hottest meals.

For hosts still in a quandary about which beers or wines to offer, why not present a number of selections to your guests and have them decide — by tasting them all — which wines and beers go best with the fiery foods being served? Two to include are our sangrias (different in taste as well as in color), Red Wine Sangria and White Wine Sangria.

AFTER-DINNER COOL-DOWNS

Believe it or not, some chile addicts believe that every course of the meal should burn. After peppery cocktails, fiery appetizers, spicy soup, and three different incendiary entrees, they have the nerve to serve jalapeño sorbet for dessert. Fortunately, the vast majority of chile cooks believe that enough is enough and consider a soothing cool-down to be the perfect finish for a fiery feast.

As with beers and wines, a debate rages over precisely which drinks actually tame the heat of chiles. Recommendations range from ice water to hot tea to lemon juice to one of our favorites, Scotch on the rocks. Most of these liquids can be dismissed out of hand. Ice water is totally useless because capsaicin and water don't mix. As soon as the water leaves the mouth, the fire rages on. Hot tea is a legendary Vietnamese remedy, but there is no logical reason for it to work because it is 99 percent water. Lemon juice seems to help some people, but somehow we can't picture our guests sitting around the table sucking on lemons after a marvelous fiery feast. And as for Scotch on the rocks, well, if you drink enough of it, you soon won't care about cooling down.

Our after-dinner drinks reveal the wide range of cool-downs. The first three, Strawberry Liquado, Agua Fresca de Tamarindo, and

Mexican Hot Chocolate, hail from south of the border, where the folks know how to make a cool-down. Our version of a famous drink, Brandy Alexander Cool-Down, has been fortified with ice cream to really cut the heat.

Actually, it was East Indian cooks who perfected the solution to the problem of after-dinner cool-downs. They discovered that the most effective antidote for capsaicin is dairy products, particularly yogurt. The Indian yogurt-and-fruit drink called *lassi* is commonly served after hot curry meals; it is sweet, refreshing, and effective. No one seems to know precisely why milk, sour cream, yogurt, and ice cream cut the heat, but they do. Some experts suggest that the protein casein in the milk counteracts the capsaicin, but all we know is that it works. Included here is Mango Lassi, with one of our favorite fruits, and Lassi, Come Home — You're Frozen, with another one in a more solid form.

So there you have it, the solution to the etiquette problem of the century: what drinks to serve with fiery foods. To review the answers briefly: first, prepare the guests with peppery cocktails for the fiery food to follow; next, match the proper wines and beers to the spicy entrees; and finally, cool down with our suggested drinks for dessert. We're certain Miss Manners will approve.

TEX-MEX LIQUORS

Chiles and cumin combine here to create the olfactory essence of the Border. Almost any type of small chile pepper that you can get into the bottle will work. Be sure to taste it often and remove the chiles when it reaches the desired heat — the longer the chiles are left in, the hotter the liquor will get! Serve extremely cold, over ice, or in tomato juice for an "instant" Bloody Mary or Maria. Flavored liquors are often prepared in the Southwest with sliced jalapeños.

4 **to 6 dried chiltepin chiles, left whole**

1 **teaspoon ground cumin**

1 **liter vodka or white tequila**

Place the chiles in the vodka and let them steep for a week or more. Periodically taste the liquor and remove the chiles when the desired heat has been obtained.

Yield: 1 liter
Heat Scale: Hot

‸‸‸‸‸‸‸‸‸‸‸‸‸‸‸

A PURIST'S PERFECTLY PUNGENT BLOODY MARY

Here it is, the ultimate Bloody Mary designed for the ultimate peppery-cocktail snob. Canned tomato juice is permitted only when fresh vine-ripened tomatoes are not available.

½ teaspoon of your favorite bottled hot sauce (or more to taste)

1½ ounces fine vodka, such as Stolichnaya or Absolut

3 ounces tomato juice freshly made from vine-ripened tomatoes (or more to taste — get out your juicer!)

1 teaspoon freshly squeezed lime juice

⅛ teaspoon soy sauce

1/16 teaspoon brown sugar

1 dash salt

Freshly ground black pepper to taste

Combine all ingredients and shake with ice cubes. Serve garnished with a slice of fresh serrano or jalapeño chile.

Serves: 1
Heat Scale: Medium

‸‸‸‸‸‸‸‸‸‸‸‸‸‸

HOT TEQUILA, FROZEN MARGARITA

1½ cups spicy tequila (or the chiltepin tequila, above)

8 fresh limes, or enough to make ½ cup juice

¼ cup Cointreau or Triple Sec

Crushed ice

Prepare 4 long-stemmed goblets by rubbing the rims with a piece of lime section. Dip the goblet rims in the salt and then place the goblets in the freezer for at least 30 minutes.

Juice the limes and then place the lime juice, tequila, and Triple Sec in a blender. Add the crushed ice until the blender is half-full and then process. Taste the result, then adjust the flavor by adding more Triple Sec to make it sweeter, more lime juice to make it more tart, more tequila to increase the heat level, or more ice to decrease the heat level. Pour into the frosted goblets and garnish each with a slice of lime.

Serves: 4
Heat Scale: Mild

〰〰〰〰〰〰

TROPICAL RUM SLUSH

Rum is the favorite drink of the Caribbean, where Dave and Mary Jane travel all the time. We prefer dark rum, but any variety will work in this cooler, which is enough for a party.

1   **12-ounce can frozen orange juice**

1   **12-ounce can frozen lemonade**

1   **12-ounce can frozen limeade**

1   **16-ounce package frozen strawberries**

1   **bottle of rum (750 milliliters)**

   Water to cover

Put all of the ingredients in a one-gallon plastic container, shake, and fill with water up to 1½ inches from the top. Cover tightly, shake the container vigorously, and freeze overnight.

Scoop the mixture into chilled old-fashioned glasses and add a straw.

Serves: 16 to 20

CHIMAYO COCKTAIL

This cocktail comes from the famous restaurant Rancho de Chimayo in Chimayo, New Mexico. The area is known for its fine apple orchards, so when you re-create this drink, make sure you use premium organic apple cider. We can taste this cocktail right now — as we sit under one of the trees on the restaurant's patio, admiring the view.

¼ cup apple cider	½ jigger cassis
1 jigger gold tequila	1 teaspoon fresh lime juice

Fill an old-fashioned glass ¾ full with ice cubes. Pour the ice cubes and the drink ingredients into a cocktail shaker and shake vigorously. Pour the contents back into the old-fashioned glass. Garnish with an apple slice if desired. The cocktail can also be served chilled without the ice, but it can be fairly potent that way!

Serves: 1

∿∿∿∿∿∿∿∿∿∿

RED WINE SANGRIA

This red sangria is a refreshing and easy drink to serve at summertime festivities. Since it is prepared in advance, the host need only pour. Served in a clear glass pitcher, it is attractive enough to grace the dining table.

1 liter dry red wine	1 lemon or 2 limes, sliced very thin
1 jigger brandy	1 peach, peeled and sliced very thin
2 to 3 tablespoons sugar	
1 orange, peeled in a single long continuous strip	Club soda, chilled
Juice from 1 orange	

Pour the wine into a large glass pitcher or punch bowl. Add the remaining ingredients, except the club soda, and stir until the sugar is dissolved. Allow the mixture to stand for 1 hour before serving, then stir again before serving. Serve in tall glasses filled with ice cubes, using three parts sangria to one part chilled club soda.

Serves: 10 to 12

\~\~\~\~\~\~\~\~\~\~\~\~

WHITE WINE SANGRIA

The traditional Spanish sangrias are very fruity, but not too sweet. We suggest you try one of these two recipes, serving it chilled in a large glass pitcher. Pre-mixed, bottled sangrias tend to be overly sweet and lack the fresh-fruit sparkle.

1 **jigger brandy**	**Peel from one orange**
2 **to 3 tablespoons sugar**	**One whole orange,**
1 **cinnamon stick**	**stabbed several times**
1 **thinly sliced lemon**	**with a sharp knife**
1 **liter dry white wine**	**Club soda, chilled**
½ **cup sliced strawberries**	

Combine all the ingredients, except the club soda, and allow to marinate for several hours or overnight in the refrigerator. Serve in tall glasses filled with ice cubes, using three parts sangria to one part club soda.

Yield: 10 to 12 drinks

STRAWBERRY LIQUADO

This refreshing non-alcoholic drink is very popular in Mexico, where it is made from all kinds of exotic fruits. In the citrus *liquados,* the fruit is halved and juiced, and the rind is put in the blender along with the other ingredients — water, ice, and a bit of sugar.

1½ **cups fresh strawberries**	1 **cup water**
1½ **cups ice**	1 **tablespoon sugar**

Place all the ingredients in a blender and blend thoroughly. Serve in a tall chilled glass.

Serves: 1

∿∿∿∿∿∿∿∿∿∿∿

AGUA FRESCA DE TAMARINDO

We thank our friend Robb Walsh for this recipe. Robb says, "Agua Fresca is thirst-quenching, has more nutritive value than tea or water, and you can drink lots of it without worrying about caffeine or alcohol." His kids drink it by the gallon to cool off during the hot Austin summers.

½ **pound tamarind beans**	1 **gallon water**
¾ **cup honey or sugar (use**	
more or less to taste)	

Rinse the beans and drain them. Put them in a soup pot and add enough water to cover them. Cook at a low boil for 10 minutes.

Mash the softened beans vigorously with a potato masher. Strain the coffee-colored liquid into a one-gallon container, throwing away the seeds and outer pods as you go.

Add the sugar or honey while the liquid is still hot. Place it in a 1-gallon container; add water to fill the container. Refrigerate and serve over more or less ice to make it as strong or as weak as you like it.

Yield: 1 gallon

~~~~~~~~~~~~~~~~

MEXICAN HOT CHOCOLATE

If you have never tried this Mexican-style hot chocolate, indulge yourself. It is quite rich and loaded with milk and cream, so save it for a sweet "splurge" occasion. In Mexico the chocolate is beaten with a *molinillo,* a wooden utensil that is quickly twirled between the palms of the hands to mix and create a froth on the chocolate.

½	cup sugar	¼	teaspoon grated nutmeg
2	tablespoons flour	6	cups low-fat milk
⅓	cup cocoa	1	teaspoon vanilla extract
1½	cups cold water	2	cups half-and-half
¼	teaspoon salt		Cinnamon sticks
1	teaspoon cinnamon		(optional)
¾	teaspoon ground cloves		

Combine the first 8 ingredients in a heavy saucepan over a low heat, whisking occasionally. Add the 6 cups of milk and scald the mixture, whisking continuously and making sure the mixture does not boil. Add the vanilla and the cream, continuing to heat and whisk until a froth appears and the milk is heated through. Serve in warm cups, garnishing with a whole cinnamon stick if desired.

Serves: 10 to 12 (depending on the size of the cups)

BRANDY ALEXANDER COOL-DOWN

A variation on a traditional cocktail, this ice cream delight doubles as both a soothing cool-down and a dessert drink.

1	ounce brandy	2	scoops vanilla ice cream, slightly softened
1	ounce brown crème de cacao		Dash of nutmeg

Place all ingredients in a blender and process. Serve in dessert glasses.

Serves: 2

∿∿∿∿∿∿∿∿∿∿∿∿

MANGO LASSI

This refreshing dessert drink originated in India, where it is often served after a meal of fiery hot curries. Fruits such as pineapple, strawberries, or peaches may be added to or substituted for the mango.

2	cups plain yogurt	Pulp of two ripe mangos
2	cups buttermilk (or substitute milk)	Juice of one lemon
		1 teaspoon sugar

Place all the ingredients in a blender and process until smooth. Serve over ice, or freeze until slushy and then serve.

Serves: 4

LASSI, COME HOME — YOU'RE FROZEN

This additional refreshing Indian concoction can be served as a drink or as a dessert — just freeze the mixture a little longer. Almost any combination of fruit will work well.

½ **cup chilled buttermilk**

½ **cup strawberry yogurt or other fruit-flavored yogurt**

¼ **cup fresh strawberries, washed and drained**

½ **teaspoon freshly squeezed lemon juice**

1 **teaspoon sugar (optional)**

Place all the ingredients in a blender and blend until smooth. Pour into a container and freeze for about 30 minutes until slushy. Break up the mixture lightly with a spoon and pour it into a chilled glass, or freeze it longer and serve in a chilled dessert dish.

Serves: 1

▼▲▼▲▼▲▼▲▼▲▼▲▼▲▼▲▼▲▼▲▼

Spicy Beers in History

Happy hour is not exactly a new concept. In fact, it has been a mainstay of mankind for more than 10,000 years! Well, maybe not in its current form — no pretzel fossils have been found — but partaking of a few spicy brews has held an important place in history.

The earliest known beer drinkers were the Pleistocene hunter-gatherers, who became cooperative farmers in order to harvest wheat to make — yep, that's right — beer. These folks liked to add a little zip to their beers by putting pepper-like plants in the village vats.

The Egyptians brewed no fewer than eight varieties of hot beers, though they did not use *Capsicum* peppers to spice things up. Cumin and the equivalent of modern-day horseradish were their condiments of choice. During the Greco-Roman period, beer suffered from a bit of bad PR. Known as *zythos,* beer was thought to be a cause of leprosy.

Luckily, things took a turn for the better with the Vikings, who introduced ale-style beer. They did use black pepper in their beer to tantalize the tastebuds, but the Norse spice of choice was garlic.

From the Aztecs (who were allowed to get as drunk as they wished after age 52 — but not many of them lived that long) to Columbus, to the fathers of the early church in Europe who brewed a hot and spicy beer, thought to be hallucinogenic (served at fundraising functions only), hot and spicy suds have made their mark on history.

Spicy and Healthy

C hile peppers don't have to be healthy to be fun to eat, but, fortunately, they are. In fact, they have quite a long history as a folk remedy for all kinds of ailments, from anorexia to vertigo. Some of the more scientifically recognized medical applications of chile peppers include treatments for asthma, arthritis, blood clots, cluster headaches, post-herpetic neuralgia (shingles), and severe burns.

BURNING CALORIES

Chile peppers contain only a few calories (37 per 100 grams of green chile, about 3½ ounces), and possibly have the ability to burn off those calories and others as well. This intriguing possibility comes from researchers at Oxford Polytechnic Institute in England, who conducted an experiment in TEF, an abbreviation for "thermic effects of food." Twelve volunteers ate identical 766-calorie meals. On one day, three grams each of chile powder and mustard were added to the meals; on the next day, nothing was added. On the days when chile and mustard were added, the volunteers burned between 4 and 76 additional calories; the average was 45.

The researchers concluded that the test was "a possible lead to a different approach to weight reduction," but also warned that the effect had been demonstrated in only one small test. They also cautioned that 6 grams (⅕ ounce) of the chile-mustard mixture "may be a large amount for the average American. If you are used to Mexican, Spanish, or Indian food, though, it's reasonable."

A possible explanation for the process is the fact that certain hot spices — especially chiles — temporarily speed up the body's metabolic rate. After eating, the metabolic rate increases anyway — a phenomenon known as "diet-induced thermic effect." But chiles boost that effect by a factor of 25, which seems to indicate that increasing the amount of chile in a recipe could reduce the effective caloric content — provided, of course, that one does not drink more beer to counter the added heat.

Another intriguing possibility has been suggested by T. George Harris, who wrote in *American Health* magazine that chiles stimulate the tastebuds but not the sense of smell. Thus they "perk up food without adding fat." Harris added that he formerly made jokes about hot pepper diets, but now, "over the last couple of years, chile peppers have begun to emerge as the nutritional heroes of the future."

GREEN AND RED VITAMINS

Most of the research on the dietary properties of hot peppers has addressed the New Mexican pod types because they are consumed more as a food than as a condiment. The long green pods are harvested, roasted, and peeled, and are stuffed or made into sauces. Some of the green pods are allowed to turn red on the bush; after harvesting, the red chiles are used as the primary ingredient in red chile sauces. The green chiles are quite high in vitamin C, with about twice the amount, by weight, found in citrus fruits; dried red chiles contain more vitamin A than carrots. Vitamin C is one of the least stable of all the vitamins; it is broken down chemically by heat, by exposure to air, by being dissolved in water, and by dehydration. Vitamin A, however, is one of the most stable vitamins and is not affected by canning, cooking, or time.

A high percentage of the vitamin C in fresh green chiles is retained in the canned and frozen products, but the vitamin C content drops dramatically in the dried red pods and powder. Each 100 grams of fresh ripe chile pods contain 369 milligrams of vitamin C, which diminishes by more than half to 154 milligrams in the dried red pods. Red chile powder contains less than 3 percent of the vitamin C of ripe pods, a low 10 milligrams.

The amount of vitamin A increases dramatically as the pod turns red and dries, from 770 units per 100 grams of green pods to 77,000 in freshly processed dried red pods. This hundredfold rise in vitamin A content is the result of increasing carotene, the chemical that produces the orange and red colors of ripe peppers. The recommended daily allowances for these vitamins are 5,000 International Units for A and 60 milligrams for C. These allowances can be satisfied daily by eating about a teaspoonful of red chile sauce for A and about an ounce of fresh green chile for C.

ADDITIONAL BENEFITS

Each 100 grams of green chile contain less than 0.2 gram of fat — a very low amount. Since no cholesterol is found in vegetable products, peppers are free of it. The fiber content of fresh hot peppers is fairly high (between 1.3 and 2.3 grams per 100 grams of chile), and many of the dishes prepared with them include starchy ingredients such as beans, pasta, and tortillas. And the sugar in chiles is in the form of healthy complex carbohydrates.

Fresh green chile contains only 3.5 to 5.7 milligrams of sodium per 100 grams — a very low amount. We suggest that chile peppers can be very useful for the low-sodium dieter. The substitution of hot peppers for salt makes gustatory sense because the pungency of the peppers counteracts the blandness imposed on the meal by salt restrictions. In other words, the heat masks the absence of salt. We have included our recipe for a spicy salt substitute, Herbal-Chile Salt Substitute (p. 9).

However, canned green chile peppers should be avoided because of the salt used in the canning process, which can be over 100 times the amount in fresh or frozen chiles. For people on a potassium-restricted diet, the opposite is true: canned chiles have one half the potassium content of fresh ones. Some experts blame this anomaly on the hot-lye-bath method of removing the tough pepper skins, a technique that provides additional sodium by absorption and reduces the potassium through leaching. It should be noted that some processors

have switched to a high-pressure steam treatment to remove skins —
a far healthier and tastier method.

MEAT SUBSTITUTES

There are basically two types of meat substitutes — those made with
soy and those made with gluten, a protein found in wheat. There are
several types of soy and one basic type of gluten — seitan — that
resemble meat when prepared properly.

Soft tofu is perfect for soups and sauces. Japanese varieties include
Kinugoshi and Silken. This type of tofu doesn't absorb flavor really well,
and must be drained thoroughly if it is to be used in a stir-fry. Chinese
"soft" tofu is firmer than Japanese Kinugoshi tofu, but still has that
smooth and creamy texture.

Regular tofu is pressed longer than soft tofu to remove more of
the water. Both Chinese and Japanese regular tofu are fairly firm, making them ideal for stir-fries or casseroles. Firm and extra-firm tofu have
been pressed to obtain an even lower water content. This type has a
pronounced skin on the outside and a grainier texture inside. The firm
tofu is full of nutrients, and is the best choice for dishes that call for
large pieces of tofu.

Often called "wheat meat," gluten is cooked into seitan, a staple
of non-meat-eating people around the world. Seitan is a chameleon of
sorts, changing flavors according to the spices and ingredients with
which it is combined. Thus it is a great substitute ingredient in many
meat recipes, since it can take on many of the tastes and textures of
the actual meat dish it is replicating.

However, the way seitan is cooked is directly related to how good it
tastes. Melissa notes, "I must admit that my first experience with seitan was not a very positive one. In fact, I thought it was pronounced
Satan, because in my estimation it tasted liked hell! I am happy to
report that since my first experience, I have had many seitan dishes
that were absolutely heavenly!" Dave's first experience with seitan was
much better. He first tasted it at A Taste of Thailand restaurant in
Des Moines, Iowa. The seitan was used in a spicy Thai salad and Dave
actually believed it was meat until he was told differently.

We would be remiss if we did not mention that making your own
seitan is fairly time-consuming; we have included a recipe for dedicated

cooks. However, seitan is available commercially in jars, in boxes, canned, and frozen if you have more money than time.

A wide variety of meat substitutes is available on the market, such as soy nuggets, nutburger mixes (in flavors including barbecue and pizza), lasagne (in Canadian bacon and chicken filet flavors), Tex-Mex tempeh, seitan (in roast beef and chicken flavors), and soybean pastes of every kind.

DAIRY PRODUCT SUBSTITUTES

Of course, there are numerous low-fat dairy products on the market, if the cook wants only to reduce fat levels in food. However, some people are either allergic to dairy products or object to eating them. For them, there is a wide variety of dairy product substitutes. They will not find an exact non-dairy match for every kind of cheese, but at least they will have some basic options.

Milk substitutes are soy-based and have names such as Eden Soy and Vita Soy. They are suitable for all baking, cooking, and drinking needs, and come in flavors such as original, vanilla, and carob. *Yogurt substitutes* are also soy-based. There are also, of course, numerous brands of cream and half-and-half substitutes, made from hydrogenated vegetable oils. *Sour cream substitutes,* available at most supermarkets, are also made from hydrogenated vegetable oils.

Butter substitutes are margarines made with a wide variety of vegetable oils, including soy oil. Soybean margarine can be used for most cooking needs. For simple frying, olive oil is an excellent butter substitute.

Cheese substitutes are usually soy- or tofu-based, with brand names such as Soya Kaas or Nu Tofu. They come in flavors such as jalapeño, mozzarella, cream cheese, garlic herb, and cheddar. There are also soy-free cheese substitutes like Almond Cheese, which is made with a non-dairy white-almond beverage. Flavors of Almond Cheese include mozzarella, jalapeño jack, and cheddar.

A Plethora
of Peppers

L iterally hundreds of varieties of peppers are grown in the world, but only a dozen or two are used for cooking in the United States. The following survey is not intended to be exhaustive (there are several books out on this subject — see Suggested Reading, p. 247), but rather a general description of the most popular peppers used in this country.

Fresh Peppers. Available from the garden or the market, fresh peppers are becoming increasingly popular as they become more commonly available. The most ubiquitous peppers are, of course, the familiar bells, which have no heat except for a variety called Mexi-Bell, which has a mild bite. The most interesting of the bell peppers are the brightly colored ones, which come in a variety of hues from yellow to orange to red to purple. They are most often used to brighten up salsas and salads. The poblano, similar in size to a bell, is a Mexican pepper with moderate to mild heat; it is often stuffed with cheese and baked.

The most readily available hot peppers in the produce sections of supermarkets are jalapeños and yellow wax peppers. The yellow wax peppers are usually mild and are stuffed or chopped for use in salsas and salads. Jalapeños — either green or fresh red — are used in a similar manner, and are often floated whole in soups or stews to provide a little extra bite, then are removed before serving. Another variety that sometimes appears fresh is the cherry pepper. This mild pepper is often pickled.

Several varieties of the long green New Mexican chiles are available fresh in the Southwest and occasionally in other locations. The No. 6-4 variety is the most commonly grown and is available from August through early November. Its hotter cousin, Sandia, is usually not seen in the green, or immature, form. The mildest New Mexican–type variety is the Anaheim, a California variety that is available most of the year. Occasionally, New Mexican chiles are identified by their grower (such as Barker) or by a regional appellation (Chimayo or Hatch or Luna County), which further confuses the issue.

All of these long green chiles must be roasted and peeled before using them in a recipe. Blistering or roasting the chile is the process of heating it to the point when the tough transparent skin is separated from the meat of the chile so it can be removed. The method is quite simple.

While processing the chiles, be sure to wear rubber gloves to protect yourself from the capsaicin, which can burn your hands and any other part of your body that you touch. Before roasting, cut a small slit in each chile close to the top, so that the steam can escape. The chiles can then be placed on a baking sheet and put directly under the broiler or on a screen on the top of the stove.

Our favorite method, which involves meditation and a bottle of Negra Modelo, is to place the pods on a charcoal grill about 5 to 6 inches from the coals. Blisters will soon indicate that the skin is separating, but be sure that the chiles are blistered all over or they will not peel properly. Immediately wrap the chiles in damp towels or place them in a plastic bag for 10 to 15 minutes — this "steams" them and loosens the skins. For crisper, less cooked chiles, plunge them into ice water to stop the cooking process.

Green chile is a low-acid fruit, and for that reason we do not recommend home canning for it. It can be done, but only by using a pressure canner and by carefully following all the manufacturer's specific instructions. We find freezing to be a much easier and more flavorful method of preservation.

If the pods are to be frozen whole (rather than chopped), they do not have to be peeled first. In fact, they are easier to peel after they have been frozen. After roasting the chiles, freeze them in the form in which you plan to use them — whole, in strips, or chopped. If you are storing them in strips or chopped, peel the pods first. A handy way to put up chopped or diced chiles is to freeze them in ice cube trays with sections. When frozen, they can be "popped" out of the trays and stored in a bag in the freezer. When making a soup or a stew, just drop in a cube! This eliminates the problems inherent in hacking apart a large slab of frozen chiles when you need just a couple of ounces.

New Mexican chiles are available fresh in season by overnight delivery (see Mail Order Sources, p. 249). They are found canned in most U.S. markets and frozen in some parts of the Southwest.

Other fresh chiles that are sometimes found in markets (especially farmer's markets) are serranos and habaneros. The serranos — smaller, thinner, and hotter than jalapeños — are the classic chiles of the Mexican *pico de gallo* fresh salsas. Habaneros, the world's hottest peppers, are lantern-shaped orange or red devils that have a unique, fruity aroma in addition to their powerful punch. Use them with caution. Generally speaking, any of the small fresh peppers may be substituted for each other; however, they are not a substitute for poblanos or the New Mexican varieties in recipes. The smaller chiles — habaneros, serranos, and jalapeños — can be frozen without processing. Wash the chiles, dry them, place them one layer deep on a cookie sheet, and freeze them. After they are frozen solid, store them in a bag. Frozen chiles will keep for nine months to a year at zero degrees Fahrenheit. All the small peppers can be frozen whole with no further processing needed, and their texture holds up surprisingly well in the freezer.

Dried Peppers. Like fresh peppers, the larger they are, the milder. The large dried peppers, such as ancho (a dried poblano) and the New Mexican varieties, are mild enough to be the principal ingredients of sauces. The smaller varieties, such as piquin, are too hot for this purpose and are generally used as condiments or in stir-frying. All dried peppers can be ground into powders (see below).

Four main large peppers are used as the base for sauces: ancho, pasilla, New Mexican, and guajillo. The ancho is a wide, dark pepper with a "raisiny" aroma. It is the only pepper that is commonly stuffed in its dried form (the pod is softened in water first). The pasilla is a long, thin, dark pepper that also has a "raisiny" or nutty aroma. Along with the ancho, it commonly appears in Mexican *mole* sauces.

The most common way to use the red New Mexican chiles is to hang them in long strings, or *ristras,* until they are ready to be used in cooking. Then they are commonly rehydrated and combined with onions, garlic, oil, spices, and water to make the classic New Mexican red chile sauce, a common topping for enchiladas in the Southwest. The guajillos, a shortened and hotter version of the New Mexican chiles, are commonly used in sauces in northern Mexico.

There are a bewildering number of small, hot pods ranging in size from that of a little fingernail (the chiltepin) to the skinny 6-inch cayenne. Some varieties include piquin, Thai, santaka, de arbol, mirasol, and tabasco. These chiles appear in stir-fry dishes, are floated in soups or stews, or are used to add heat to sauces that are too mild. A specialized dried chile that has become quite popular is the chipotle, a smoke-dried red jalapeño.

Powders. All chiles can be dried and ground into powder — and most are, including the habanero. Crushed chiles, or those coarsely ground with some of their seeds, are called *quebrado.* Coarse powders are referred to as *caribe;* the finer powders are termed *molido.* The milder powders, such as New Mexican, can also be used as a base for sauces, but the hotter powders such as cayenne and piquin are used when heat is needed more than flavor. In our homes, we actually have more powders available than whole pods because the powders are concentrated and take up less storage space. We store them in small, airtight bottles. The fresher the powders, the better they taste, so don't grind up too many pods. Use an electric spice mill and be sure to wear a painter's mask to protect your nose and throat from the pungent powder. The colors of the powders vary from a bright, electric red-orange (chiltepins) to light green (dried jalapeños) to a dark brown that verges on black (ancho). We love to experiment by changing the powders called for in recipes.

Other Chile Products. A vast number of foods and condiments now contain chile peppers. Quite a few of these products are handy for cooks who love all things hot and spicy and meatless. Look for chile-infused vinegars, oils, mustards, ketchups, cheeses, pickles, hot sauces, salad dressings, jams and jellies, soups, pastas, potato and corn chips, curry powders and pastes, nuts, and even candies.

Grow Your Own Chile Garden

O ur interest in hot and spicy and meatless foods was stimulated by the gardens raised by our two famililes and by the necessity of dealing with a bountiful harvest. Every year, for example, the DeWitt family grows what might be called a basic garden for most vegetables and a specialized garden for chiles.

In our basic garden we grow several varieties of tomatoes and corn, eggplants, beans, and a variety of herbs such as basil, Italian parsley, garlic, thyme, oregano, lemongrass, and cilantro. Some years we plant zucchini, tomatillos, and peas. We don't have room for root crops such as potatoes, and have no shaded areas for salad greens.

Our pride and joy is our chile garden, and it all began innocently enough. Back in the late '70s, when we first started researching and writing about chile peppers, we decided that we should include a couple of hot pepper plants. The following year we planted a few more varieties, and from then on we've continued to increase the number of plants as well as the number of different varieties of chile we grow until it's become nearly a full-time obsession. As we work on this book, for example, we are growing more than 40 different varieties of chile peppers in our garden and in containers around the yard.

Aside from our obvious madness, why are we growing so many chiles? First is our love of gardening and the challenge that all these chiles present. Many of the varieties we grow are native to humid or tropical climates — unlike Albuquerque, where 20 percent humidity is considered high. Other varieties are grown only in the shade, which is rare here in the desert. Cultivating these non-native plants in our high-altitude gardens (we're right at 5,000 feet) with the dryness, the unbelievably intense sunlight, and the high winds requires all of our ingenuity.

The second reason for our obsession is the fact that we eat chile peppers in some form every day because they taste great and add both flavor and excitement to a wide variety of foods. We constantly experiment with recipes in an attempt to discover which chiles work best with various exotic cuisines.

Finally, we continue to expand our chile gardens in order to learn as much as possible about chiles themselves. We want to determine which chiles are the easiest to grow, which are the tastiest, which produce the most fruit, and which are the hottest.

A PRACTICAL PEPPER PATCH

In addition to our goal of attempting to grow every possible variety of chile pepper, we are also interested in perfecting a practical pepper patch, one that produces the greatest number of peppers with the widest possible range of uses. To select the most useful chile peppers, we applied the following criteria: varying degrees of heat, from mild to wild; variety of preservation methods and versatility in recipes; availability of seeds; and simplicity of cultivation, especially in northern climates. Seeds for these varieties are available from local nurseries and from mail order sources (see p. 249).

About six weeks before the time to transplant seedlings into the garden, we start the seeds in plastic six-pack seedling growers, just like commercial greenhouses do. We use a vermiculite-based growing medium, rather than soil, because it allows the seedlings' roots to receive more oxygen and thus to grow faster.

The six-packs are set in trays on top of heating wire or tape to keep soil temperatures above 75 degrees, since the warmth of the soil can radically affect the germination percentage of most chile varieties. A recent comparison of germination techniques for wild chiltepin seeds revealed that heating the soil increased germination percentages from 10 percent to 80 percent.

The seedlings should be grown in full sun in a greenhouse or window so they do not become "leggy" and topple over. Some leggy seedlings can be pinched back to make a bushier plant and to ensure that leaf growth does not overwhelm stem growth. Keep the seedlings moist but not wet; overwatering will cause stem rot. It will also be necessary to fertilize the plants after they have put out their first true leaves. We use an all-purpose water-soluble fertilizer (15-30-15), ¼ teaspoon to a gallon of water, every time we water our seedlings. When growing seedlings in the house, remember that cats love to graze on tender young plants — which will not harm the cats but will destroy the chiles.

Chile peppers should not be set out in the garden until after the last frost, and ideally should not be set out until the temperature of the garden soil 4 inches below the surface reaches 65 degrees. Before transplanting, the seedlings should be "hardened off" by placing the trays outside for a few hours each day during warm, sunny days. The constant movement of the seedlings caused by light breezes will strengthen the stems and prepare the plants for the rigors of the garden. Chile pepper gardeners living in particularly chilly regions should wait until the plants blossom before planting them in the garden.

If the garden plot is to be irrigated, use a shovel to make rows and furrows, and then set the chile pepper plants 2 feet apart. It is possible to cram more plants into the garden, or to reduce the square footage used. This size and spacing worked best for us mainly because it enabled us to harvest the pods without stomping on the plants. Some gardeners place the chiles as close as 1 foot apart so the plants will shade each other and protect the fruit from sunburn. If necessary, protect the young chile plants from freak frosts and cutworms by covering them with glass or plastic jars at night.

After the chiles have been transplanted, the garden should be thoroughly mulched. Use several layers of newspaper in hot climates, or black plastic film in cool summer climates. In locations where summer temperatures are regularly in the 90s, black plastic in a garden can raise the temperature in that microclimate so high that the plants will stop flowering. Layers of newspaper weighted down with soil reflect sunlight, hold water, and provide additional organic material for the soil after they disintegrate.

Chiles need regular water and plenty of it, but overwatering is the biggest mistake of the home gardener. Well-drained soil is the key here, and the first indication of overwatering is water standing in the garden for any length of time. Some wilting of the plants in the hot summer sun is normal, and is not always an indication that the plants need water.

A high-nitrogen fertilizer encourages foliage growth, but it should be discontinued after flowering. Some growers encourage root growth by adding a teaspoon of phosphate 2 inches below the planting hole during transplanting.

In order to set fruit, the plants require daytime temperatures between 65 and 80 degrees and night temperatures above 55 degrees. Flowering decreases during the hottest months of the summer, and in fact, extremely hot or dry conditions will cause the blossoms to drop off the plant. However, in the early fall, flowering picks up again; in northern regions, though, fall blooms are unlikely to yield fruit. In most locations, the first hard frost will kill the plants, and at that point all the remaining pods should be removed.

Chile plants and pods are assaulted by a large number of insect pests, including aphids, beetles, borers, bugs, flies, hoppers, miners, mites, scales, and worms. Interestingly enough, chiles can protect themselves when the hottest pods available are transformed into an organic insecticide. Take 8 ounces of the hottest pods in the garden and liquefy them in a blender with a small onion, 6 cloves of garlic, 1 tablespoon of natural soap, 3 tablespoons of pyrethrum powder, and 2 or more cups of water. Strain the mixture through cheesecloth and dilute with water to the desired consistency for use in a sprayer. Spray the tops and bottoms of the pepper leaves every 48 hours and most insect pests should be controlled, if not terminated.

We are often asked if cultivation techniques can alter the amount of capsaicin in the pods and make the chiles hotter or milder. The amount of capsaicin in chiles is theoretically genetically fixed, which means that the plants will breed true to their heat levels under ideal conditions. However, undue stress on the plants in the form of heat, drought, or flooding can dramatically increase the heat levels, according to researchers at New Mexico State University. There is no known gardening procedure for decreasing the capsaicin in the pods — that can only be done in the kitchen with diluting or buffering techniques.

HARVESTING THE HEAT

We recommend the technique of staggered harvesting, which means that the chiles in the garden can be used all year long. Usually the first chiles available are those that are small and used green in fresh salsas — the serranos, the jalapeños, and the young green pods of other varieties such as the habanero.

Some chiles, especially the New Mexican varieties, can be eaten or processed as soon as they are about 4 inches long, or they can be allowed to turn red before picking and drying. However, a few varieties, such as cayenne and santaka chiles, are generally used only in their dried state.

It is important to continue harvesting the ripe pods as they mature. If the pods are allowed to remain on the plant, few new ones will form, whereas if the pods are continuously harvested, the plants will produce great numbers of chiles. The best time to pick chiles for drying is when they first start to turn red. This timing will stimulate the plant to further production, and the harvested chiles can be strung to dry and will turn bright red.

Haphazard harvesting can result in waste, so careful planning is essential to ensure maximum efficiency for the practical chile pepper patch. Chiles can be picked when they are green or when they are fully mature (red). It's best to be patient because chiles picked too early have not had time to develop their full flavor. Choose pods that have smooth, shiny skins and are firm to the touch. A good rule to follow is that if the pod comes off the stem easily, the chile is ready. If you have to tug on the pod, it is too early to pick it. The small chiles do not have to be peeled or processed in any way before being used. They can be picked, washed, and used in any recipe.

Drying is the oldest and most common way to preserve chile pods and works well for most chiles — except the very meaty ones such as jalapeños, which are smoke-dried and called *chipotle*. For hundreds of years, New Mexicans have been stringing chiles into *ristras* and hanging them in the sun to dry.

To dry chiles, select those that have turned red or another mature color. If the chile is picked before it starts to turn, it is very likely that it never will. Avoid any pods that have black spots, since these will mold and rot. In warm, arid climates, string the chiles through the stems and hang until dry. In cool, moist climates, the best bet for drying chiles is to use a food dehydrator. Dried chiles can be reconstituted in a variety of ways. They can be roasted very lightly on a griddle, they can be fried in a little oil until they puff and reconstitute slightly, or they can be soaked in hot water for 15 to 20 minutes.

Roasted and peeled green chiles can also be dried. String the chiles together, cover with cheesecloth, and dry in a well-ventilated location. One ounce of this chile *pasado* (dried green chile) is equivalent to 10 to 12 fresh chile pods. Chile peppers can also be pickled or made into vinegars, oils, salsas, and sauces.

Most gardeners will not grow as many plants as we do, but their harvests are bound to be abundant. We confess that we still have not figured out what to do with our proliferation of pungent pods. Our friends, our relatives, our neighbors, and even the occasional stranger we accost simply can't absorb our surplus in the good years. We grow only a few plants of each variety, and thus never wind up with large enough quantities of any one to sell at the farmer's market. Also, many of our chiles are strange to New Mexicans accustomed to three or four varieties at the most. Since all of us seem to be gradually eliminating other vegetables from our gardens in order to squeeze in more chile pepper plants, it is a little scary to peer 10 years into the future and predict what our gardens will be like then. Who knows where this fiery obsession will lead?

Suggested Reading

The Brilliant Bean, Sally and Martin Stone. New York: Bantam, 1988.

The Complete Book of Food, Carol Ann Rinzler. New York: World Almanac, 1987.

Cooking with Gluten and Seitan, Dorothy R. Bates and Colby Wingate. Summertown, TN: The Book Publishing Co., 1993.

The Food Lover's Companion, Sharon Tyler Herbst. New York: Barron's, 1990.

The Glorious Noodle, Linda Merinoff. New York: Poseidon, 1986.

The Great Chile Book, Mark Miller. Berkeley, CA: Ten Speed Press, 1991.

The Harvest Gardener, Susan McClure. Pownal, VT: Garden Way, 1992.

History of Food, Maguelonne Toussaint-Samat. Cambridge, MA: Blackwell Publishers, 1992.

The Pepper Garden, Dave DeWitt and Paul Bosland. Berkeley, CA: Ten Speed Press, 1993.

The Secret Life of Food, Martin Elkhort. Los Angeles: Jeremy P. Tarcher, 1991.

The Total Tomato, Fred Dubose. New York: Harper Colophon, 1985.

The Whole Chile Pepper Book, Dave DeWitt and Nancy Gerlach. Boston: Little, Brown, 1990.

The Whole Foods Encyclopedia, Rebecca Wood. New York: Prentice Hall, 1988.

A World of Salads, Rosalie Swedlin. New York: Holt, Rinehart and Winston, 1980.

Mail Order Sources

Many of the products mentioned in the recipes are carried by the companies listed below.

***Chile Pepper* Magazine**
P.O. Box 80780
Albuquerque, NM 87198
(800) 9595-HOT (959-5468)
The magazine of spicy world
  cuisine.

Colorado Spice Company
5030 Nome St., Unit A
Denver, CO 80239
(303) 373-0141
Spices, herbs, and chile peppers.

Dean and DeLuca
Mail Order Department
560 Broadway
New York, NY 10012
(212) 431-1691
Exotic herbs and spices from
  around the world.

Don Alfonso Foods
P.O. Box 201988
Austin, TX 78720
(800) 456-6100
Imported Mexican chiles; chipotles
  in adobo in glass containers.

Le Saucier
Faneuil Hall Marketplace
Boston, MA 02109
(617) 227-9649
Sauces, salsas, and condiments
  from all over the world.

Nancy's Specialty Market
P.O. Box 327
Wye Mills, MD 21679

(800) 462-6291
Spices, herbs, hot sauces,
  coconut extract, coconut milk, curry
  pastes, Indian pickles and chutneys.

**Old Southwest Trading
  Company**
P.O. Box 7545
Albuquerque, NM 87194
(505) 836-0168
New Mexican and Mexican
  chiles; sauces and salsas;
  Southwest gifts.

Santa Fe Exotix
500 N. Guadalupe, De Vargas
  Center, Ste. G-473
Santa Fe, NM 87501
(505) 988-7063
Unusual bottled salsas.

Shepherd's Garden Seeds
6116 Highway 9
Felton, CA 95108
(408) 335-5216
Chile pepper and exotic
  vegetable seeds.

**Stonewall Chile Pepper
  Company**
P.O. Box 241
Stonewall, TX 78671
(800) 232-2995
Habanero products, including
  salsas and ketchup.

INDEX